THE SILENT LIFE

BOOKS BY THOMAS MERTON

THE
SILENT
LIFE

BY THOMAS MERTON

Farrar, Straus & Giroux • *New York*

© 1957 by The Abbey of Our Lady of Gethsemani

Library of Congress catalog card number 56-6164

Ex Parte Ordinis
Nihil Obstat: Fr. M. Augustine Westland, O.C.S.O.
Fr. M. Paul Bourne, O.C.S.O.
Imprimi Potest: Fr. M. Gabriel Sortais, O.C.S.O.,
Abbot General
Nihil Obstat: John A. Goodwine, Censor Librorum
Imprimatur: FRANCIS CARDINAL SPELLMAN,
Archbishop of New York
New York, September 7, 1956

Published simultaneously in Canada

Printed in the United States of America

Fifth printing, 1980

CONTENTS

PROLOGUE

What Is a Monk?

A monk is a man who has been called by the Holy Spirit to relinquish the cares, desires and ambitions of other men, and devote his entire life to seeking God. The concept is familiar. The reality which the concept signifies is a mystery. For in actual fact, no one on earth knows precisely what it means to "seek God" until he himself has set out to find Him. No man can tell another what this search means unless that other is enlightened, at the same time, by the Spirit speaking within his own heart. In the end, no one can seek God unless he has already begun to find Him. No one can find God without having first been found by Him. A monk is a man who seeks God because he has been found by God. In short, a monk is a "man of God."

Since all men were created by God that they might find Him, all men are called in some sense to be "men of God." But not all are called to be monks. A monk is therefore one who is called to give himself exclusively and perfectly to the one thing necessary for all men—the search for God. It is permissible for others to seek God by a road less direct, to lead a good life in the world, to raise a Christian family. The monk puts these things aside, though they may be good. He travels to God by the direct path, *recto tramite*. He withdraws from "the world." He gives himself entirely to prayer, meditation, study, labor, penance, under the eyes of God. The monk is distinguished even from other religious vocations by the fact that he is essentially and exclusively dedicated to seeking God, rather than seeking souls for God.

Let us face the fact that the monastic vocation tends to present itself to the modern world as a problem and as a scandal.

In a basically religious culture, like that of India, or of Japan, the monk is more or less taken for granted. When all society is oriented beyond the mere transient quest of business and pleasure, no one is surprised that men should devote their lives to an invisible God. In a materialistic culture which is fundamentally irreligious the monk is incomprehensible because he "produces nothing." His life appears to be completely useless. Not even Christians have been exempt from anxiety over this apparent "uselessness" of the monk, and we are familiar with the argument that the monastery is a kind of dynamo which, though it does not "produce" grace, procures this infinitely precious spiritual commodity for the world.

The first Fathers of monasticism were concerned with no such arguments, valid though they may be in their proper context. The Fathers did not feel that the search for God was something that needed to be defended. Or rather, they saw that if men did not realize in the first place that God was to be sought, no other defence of monasticism would avail with them.

Is God, then, to be sought?

The deepest law in man's being is his need for God, for life. God is Life. "In Him was life, and the life was the light of men, and the light shineth in the darkness and the darkness comprehended it not" (John 1:5). The deepest need of our darkness is to comprehend the light which shines in the midst of it. Therefore God has given us, as His first commandment: "Thou shalt love the Lord thy God with thy whole heart, and with thy whole soul and with all thy strength." The monastic life is nothing but the life of those who have taken the first commandment in deadly earnest, and have, in the words of St Benedict, "preferred nothing to the love of Christ."

But Who is God? Where is He? Is Christian monasticism a search for some pure intuition of the Absolute? A cult of the supreme Good? A worship of perfect and changeless Beauty? The very emptiness of such abstractions strikes the heart cold. The Holy One, the Invisible, the Almighty is infinitely greater and more real than any abstraction of man's devising. But He has said: "No one shall see me and live" (Exodus 33:20). Yet the monk persists in crying out with Moses: "Show me Thy face" (Exodus 33:13).

The monk, then, is one who is so intent upon the search for God that he is ready to die in order to see Him. That is why the monastic life is a "martyrdom" as well as a "paradise," a life that is at once "angelic" and "crucified."

St Paul resolves the problem: "God who commanded the light to shine out of darkness, hath shined in our hearts to give the light of the knowledge of the glory of God, in the face of Christ Jesus" (2 Corinthians 4:6).

The monastic life is the rejection of all that obstructs the spiritual rays of this mysterious light. The monk is one who leaves behind the fictions and illusions of a merely human spirituality in order to plunge himself in the faith of Christ. Faith is the light which illumines him in mystery. Faith is the power which seizes upon the inner depths of his soul and delivers him up to the action of the divine Spirit, the Spirit of liberty, the Spirit of love. Faith takes him, as the power of God took the ancient prophets, and "stands him upon his feet" (Ezechiel 2:2) before the Lord. The monastic life is life in the Spirit of Christ, a life in which the Christian gives himself entirely to the love of God which transforms him in the light of Christ.

"The Lord is a Spirit, and where the Spirit of the Lord is, there is liberty. But we all, beholding the glory of the Lord with open face, are transformed into the same image from glory to glory, as by the Spirit of the Lord" (Corinthians 3:17-18). What St Paul has said of the inner life of every Christian becomes in all truth the main objective of the monk, living in his solitary cloister. In seeking Christian perfection the monk seeks the fullness of the Christian life, the complete maturity of Christian faith. For him, "to live is Christ."

In order to be free with the freedom of the children of God, the monk gives up his own will, his power to own property, his love of ease and comfort, his pride, his right to raise a family, his freedom to dispose of his time as he pleases, to go where he likes and to live according to his own judgment. He lives alone, poor, in silence. Why? Because of what he believes. He believes the word of Christ, Who has promised: "There is no man who has left house or parents or brethren or wife or children for the Kingdom of God's sake, who shall not receive much more in this present time, and in the world to come life everlasting" (Luke 18:29-30).

This book is a meditation on the monastic life by one who, without any merit of his own, is privileged to know that life from the inside. If there is anything of value in these pages, it comes from no special talent of the author, who seeks only to speak as the mouthpiece of a tradition centuries old, and as an unworthy descendent of St Benedict and the First Apostles, to whom all monks look back as their spiritual Fathers.

As there is nothing more distasteful than the attempt to publicize the monastic life, so too there are few things more gratifying than the hope that one may make known something of the inner mystery of a life so rich in the mercy and the goodness of God.

In these pages, we shall first consider some of the main aspects of the monastic life as such, and then go on to speak of the more important monastic Orders that flourish in the Church at the present day. Our intention is to give some idea of the monastic spirit as it is found among the cenobites (Benedictines and Cistercians) and the hermits (Carthusians and Camaldolese).

In speaking of the loftiness of the monastic ideal and of the excellence of this particular way of life, we nowhere mean to give the impression that the monastic Orders are by their very nature superior to other religious institutes for, after all, the chief dignity of the monk lies in the fact that he has abandoned competition and the quest for human glory and is content to be the last of all. To state it more accurately, the monk has no standard by which to compare himself with other religious. His eyes are not turned towards the battlefields in the plain, they gaze out upon the desert where Christ will once again appear at the right hand of the Father, coming in glory upon the clouds of heaven.

The monastic horizon is clearly the horizon of the desert. Even when writing for Christians in the world, or painting the image of Christ the Ruler of all for a parish or community, the monk has his face turned toward the desert. His ears are attuned not to the echoes of the apostolate that storms the city of Babylon but to the silence of the far mountains on which the armies of God and the enemy confront one another in a mysterious battle, of which the battle in the world is only a pale reflection.

The monastic Church is the Church of the wilderness, the woman who has fled into the desert from the dragon that seeks to devour the infant Word. She is the Church who, by her silence, nourishes and protects the seed of the Gospel that is sown by the Apostles in the hearts of the faithful. She is the Church who, by her prayer, gains strength for the Apostles themselves, so often harassed by the monster. The Monastic Church is the one who flees to a special place prepared for her by God in the wilderness, and hides her face in the Mystery of the divine silence, and prays while the great battle is being fought between earth and heaven.

Her flight is not an evasion. If the monk were able to understand what goes on inside him, he would be able to say how well he knows that the battle is being fought in his own heart.

I

THE MONASTIC PEACE

1. *Puritas Cordis* [Purity of Heart]

We have defined a monk as a man who leaves everything else in order to seek God. But this definition is not going to mean much unless we also define the search for God. And that is not an easy matter. For God is at the same time, as one of the Fathers said, everywhere and nowhere. How can I find One Who is nowhere? If I find Him, I myself will also be nowhere. And if I am nowhere, how shall I be able to say that I am still "I"? Will I still exist to rejoice in having found Him?

How can I find Him Who is everywhere? If He is everywhere, He is indeed close to me, and with me, and in me: perhaps He will turn out to be, in some mysterious way, my own self. But then, again, if He and I are one, then is there an "I" that can rejoice in having found Him?

God, says philosophy, is both immanent and transcendent. By His immanence He lives and acts in the intimate metaphysical depths of everything that exists. He is "everywhere." By His transcendence He is so far above all being, that no human and limited concept can contain and exhaust His Being, or even signify it except by analogy. He is so far above all created being that His Being and finite being are not even said to "be" in the same univocal sense. Compared with God, created being "is not"; again, compared with created being, God "is not." For He is so far above His creation that the concept of Being, applied to Him, means something basically different from what it means when applied to everything else. In this way, God "is nowhere."

The monk is one who is called by God to enter into this dilemma and this mystery. But it is less complicated for him, because he is not usually a philosopher. He seeks God not by speculation, but by a way more likely to find Him—the obscure and secret path of theological faith.

The monk, then, is one who has heard God speak the words He spoke once through the Prophet: "I will espouse thee to me in faith, and thou shalt know that I am the Lord" (Osee, 2:20).

God is said to be "found" by the soul that is

united to Him in a bond as intimate as marriage. And this bond is a union of spirits, in faith. Faith, here, means complete fidelity, the complete gift and abandonment of oneself. It means perfect trust in a hidden God. It implies submission to the gentle but inscrutable guidance of His infinitely hidden Spirit. It demands the renunciation of our own lights and our own prudence and our own wisdom and of our whole "self" in order to live in and by His Spirit. "He that is joined to the Lord," says St Paul, "is one Spirit" (1 Corinthians, 6:17).

To be one with One Whom one cannot see is to be hidden, to be nowhere, to be no one: it is to be unknown as He is unknown, forgotten as He is forgotten, lost as He is lost to the world which nevertheless exists in Him. Yet to live in Him is to live by His power, to reach from end to end of the universe in the might of His wisdom, to rule and form all things in and with Him. It is to be the hidden instrument of His Divine action, the minister of His redemption, the channel of His mercy, and the messenger of His infinite Love.

Monastic solitude, poverty, obedience, silence and prayer dispose the soul for this mysterious destiny in God. Asceticism itself does not produce divine union as its direct result. It only disposes the soul for union. The various practices of monastic asceticism are more or less valuable

3

to the monk in proportion as they help him to accomplish the inner and spiritual work that needs to be done to make his soul poor, and humble, and empty, in the mystery of the presence of God. When ascetic practices are misused, they serve only to fill the monk with himself and to harden his heart in resistance to grace. That is why all monastic asceticism centers in the two great virtues of humility and obedience which cannot be practiced as they ought to be practiced, if they do not empty a man of himself.

Humility detaches the monk first of all from that absorption in himself which makes him forget the reality of God. It detaches him from that fixation upon his own will which makes him ignore and disobey the eternal Will in which alone reality is to be found. It gradually pulls down the edifice of illusory projects which he has erected between himself and reality. It strips him of the garment of spurious ideals which he has woven to disguise and beautify his own imaginary self. It finds and saves him in the midst of a hopeless conflict against the rest of the universe—saves him in this conflict by a salutary "despair" in which he renounces at last his futile struggle to make himself into a "god." When he achieves this final renunciation he plunges through the center of his humility to find himself at last in the Living God.

The victory of monastic humility is the victory of the real over the unreal—a victory in which false human ideals are discarded and the divine "ideal" is attained, is experienced, is grasped and possessed, not in a mental image but in the present and concrete and existential reality of our life. The victory of monastic humility is a triumph of life in which, by the integration of thought and action, idealism and reality, prayer and work, the monk finds that he now lives perfectly, and fully, and fruitfully in God. Yet God does not appear. The monk is not outwardly changed. He has no aureola. He is still a frail and limited human being. The externals of his life are the same as they always were. Prayer is the same, work is the same, the monastic community is the same, but everything has been changed from within and God is, to use St Paul's expression, "all in all."

By monastic humility, the monk ceases to swim against the stream of life, gives up the sinister unconscious struggle which he has always waged to assert himself against the will of others, to resist the desires of his superiors, to impose himself upon his brothers as a distinct and superior being. He now no longer speaks and acts in his own name, but in the name of his eternal Father. Like Jesus, he finds his meat and nourishment in doing the will of "Him Who sent me." And with Jesus he can say: "He that sent me is with me, and he hath not left me alone, for I always do the things that please Him" (John, 8:29).

This does not mean that the monk becomes incapable of sin. Indeed, his weakness and helplessness have shown him that it is impossible for him to realize, on earth, a state of absolute moral perfection. Like St Paul he is compelled to say: "I am delighted with the law of God according to my inward man, but I see another law in my members fighting against the law of my mind" (Romans, 7:22-23). But also with St Paul he can declare: "I know that to them that love God all things work together unto good" (*id*. 8:28) and "Gladly will I glory in my infirmities that the power of Christ may dwell in me. For which cause I please myself in my infirmities, in reproaches for Christ. For when I am weak, then am I powerful" (2 Corinthians, 12:9-10).

The victory of monastic humility is the full acceptance of God's hidden action in the weakness and ordinariness and unsatisfactoriness of our own everyday lives. It is the acceptance of our own incompleteness, in order that He may make us complete in His own way. It is joy in our emptiness, which can only be filled by Him. It is peace in our own unfruitfulness which He Himself makes immensely fruitful without our being able to understand how it is done.

But for humility to take possession of his soul, the monk must finally and completely renounce all the worry and agitation with which he strives to hide his limitations from himself and disguise his faults as virtues. Perfection is not for those who strive to feel and look and act as if they were perfect: it is only for those who are fully aware that they are sinners, like the rest of men, but sinners loved and redeemed and changed by God. Perfection is not for those who isolate themselves in ivory towers of an imaginary fault-lessness, but only for those who risk the tarnishing of their supposed interior purity by plunging fully into life as it must inevitably be lived in this imperfect world of ours: life with its difficulties, its temptations, its disappointments and its dangers. Perfection, too, is not for those who live for themselves alone and occupy themselves exclusively with the embellishment of their own souls. Christian sanctity is not merely a matter of "recollection" or "interior prayer." Sanctity is love: the love of God above all other beings and the love of our brother in God. Such love ultimately demands the complete forgetfulness of ourselves.

And yet, the monk is traditionally one who leaves the world, flies from the company of men and seeks to purify his soul by living alone with the angels. Does he not thereby run the risk of losing all contact with reality and falling away from the life-giving union with his brothers in Christ, by which alone he can be sanctified? Is not the monastic life, then, an escape into sterility, a flight from the responsibility of living? Does it not so completely diminish and restrict a man's life that he ceases to live and spends his days vegetating in the throes of a pious delusion?

It must be admitted that every vocation has its professional hazards and the monk who loses sight of the meaning of his monastic calling may well waste his life in sterile self-preoccupation. But the meaning of the monk's flight from the world is precisely to be sought in the fact that the "world" (in the sense in which it is condemned by Christ) is the society of those who live exclusively for themselves. To leave the "world" then, is to leave oneself first of all and begin to live for others. The man who lives "in the world but not of it" is one who, in the midst of life, with all its crises, forgets himself to live for those he loves. The monastery aims to create an atmosphere most favorable for selflessness. If some of the monks make a bad use of their opportunity and become selfish, it is because they have physically left "the world" while bringing its spirit with them into the monastery in their hearts. They have not come to seek God so much as their own interests, their own profit, their own peace, their own perfection.

But now we have come to the true secret of

the monastic life and the answer to the question, what does it mean to seek God?

It means to live in Christ, to find the Father in the Son, His Incarnate Word, by sharing, through faith and the gift of self, in the obedience and the poverty and the charity of Christ.

The monastic life is not only devoted to the study of Christ, or to the contemplation of Christ, or to the imitation of Christ. The monk seeks to *become* Christ by sharing in the passion of Christ.

Life in the monastery, says Cassian, is lived "under the sacrament of the Cross" (*sub crucis sacramento*).*

But to live in the mystery of the Cross is to live in union with Christ in His "obedience unto death, even the death of the Cross" (Philippians 2, 8-9).

Many details of the monk's austere life may be relaxed by his superiors. There may be modification in his daily prayer, his manual work, his fasting, his silence: but in one thing there can be no change—in the monk's fundamental obligation to be "obedient unto death." This means

---

* Cassian quotes this expression from one of the Desert Fathers, Abbot Pinuphius, speaking to a young cenobite on his profession day: "Consider therefore the conditions of the Cross, under whose sacrament thou must live in this world henceforth, because not is it thou that livest, but He lives in thee who was crucified for thee." *Institute*, iv, 34, Migne P.L. 49:195.

that he must relinquish, if not life itself, at least his stubborn will to "live" and exist as a self-assertive and self-seeking individual. To renounce the pleasure of one's dearest illusions about oneself is to die more effectively than one could ever do by allowing himself to be killed for a clearly conceived personal ideal. Indeed, we know it is quite possible for a man to lay down his life to bear witness to his own will and to his own illusions. But the true and complete renunciation of ourselves is demanded by the monastic life. Even if our superiors seek to spare our weakness God Himself will not spare us, if we are truly seeking Him.

However, to live "under the sacrament of the Cross" is to share in the life of the Risen Christ. For when our illusions die, they give place to reality, and when our false "self" disappears, when the darkness of our self-idolatry is dispelled, then the words of the Apostle are fulfilled in us: "Arise, thou that sleepest, and Christ will enlighten thee" (Ephesians, 5:14). And again: "God who commanded the light to shine out of darkness hath shined in our hearts to give the light of the knowledge of the glory of God in the face of Christ Jesus" (2 Corinthians, 4:6).

This light of God shining in the humble soul that is empty of self, is what the Fathers called *puritas cordis*, purity of heart. Cassian said that the whole purpose of the monastic life was to lead the monk to this inner purity. All the monastic observances and virtues have this for their object.

In the words of Cassian:

It is for the sake of this purity of heart that we must do all that we do and seek all that we seek. For the sake of purity of heart we seek solitude, fasting, vigils, labors, poor clothing, reading and all the other monastic virtues. Through these practices we hope to be able to keep our heart untouched by the assaults of all the passions, and by these steps we hope to ascend to perfect love.*

He goes on to make a profound psychological observation. If, he says, we find that we are unwilling or unable to give up some particular practice or observance for the sake of some other worthy and necessary task, and if we find that when we cannot keep to our plan of observance we are sad, angry, indignant, or otherwise disturbed, it means that we are seeking these things for their own sakes and that we are therefore losing sight of our true objective which is purity of heart. For in this case the practices we follow are not purifying our heart of its selfish passions, but strengthening those very passions in our soul.

The purity of heart which Cassian describes is not so much a psychological state as a new

---

* Cassian, *Conference* 1, vii, Migne P.L. 49:489.

vel of reality. It is the condition of a soul transformed in perfect charity. Such a soul is lifted above itself and out of itself. It not only thinks and acts on a higher level, but is itself a new being, *nova creatura*.

The Fathers of the Church explained this "new being" of the soul by their doctrine that man, created in the *image* of God, has lost his *likeness* to God by becoming centered on himself. In losing his divine likeness, man has plunged into unreality for he is no longer united to the source of his reality. He still exists. He is still the "image" of his maker. But he does not have in him the life of charity which is the life of God Himself—since God is charity. Since he does not have this life in him, he is unreal, he is dead. He is not what he is supposed to be. He is a caricature of himself. An image which is nevertheless unlike what it represents is necessarily a distortion. And this distortion is, in fact, a complete spiritual opposition to the will and love of God. Made to fulfill himself by a perfect resemblance to God Who is perfect love, man destroys his potentialities by centering all his love on himself. Made to bear witness to the infinite truth and power and reality and actuality of God, in Whom all things live and move and have their being, man denies reality and turns away from truth in order to make himself the center and the *raison d'etre* of the universe.

In order to become once again "real" man must purify his heart of the darkness of unreality and illusion. But this darkness overwhelms his heart as long as he lives by his own selfish will. Light can only dawn in our hearts when we renounce our determination to rebel against the infinite will of God, accept reality as He has willed it to be, and place our wills at the service of His perfect freedom. It is when we love as He loves that we are pure, when we will what He wills, we are free. Then our eyes are opened and we can see reality as He sees it, and we can rejoice with His joy because all things are "very good" (Genesis 1:31).

The "impure" heart of fallen man is not merely a heart subject to carnal passion. "Purity" and "impurity" in this context mean something more than chastity. The "impure" heart is a heart filled with fears, anxieties, conflicts, doubts, ambivalences, hesitations, self-contradictions, hatreds, jealousies, compulsive needs and passionate attachments. All these and a thousand other "impurities" darken the inner light of the soul but they are neither its chief impurity nor the cause of its impurities. The inner, basic, metaphysical defilement of fallen man is his profound and illusory conviction that he is a god and that the universe is centered upon him. Note that this conviction *has a basis in truth*, since he sees in himself the obscure image of

13

God. What is this image? St Bernard says it is man's freedom. And so man, feeling in himself this deep, inalienable power for spiritual self-determination, this freedom to shape his own destiny by his own choice, feels himself to be indeed "godlike." This freedom comes to us from God our Father.

But although God our Father made us free, He did not make us omnipotent. We are not gods in our own right, capable of achieving everything that we desire, of creating and un-creating worlds, or commanding the adoration and service of every other spirit! We are capable of becoming perfectly godlike, in all truth, by freely receiving from God the gift of His Light, and His Love, and His Freedom in Christ, the Incarnate Logos. But in so far as we are implicitly convinced that we *ought to be omnipotent* of ourselves we usurp to ourselves a godlikeness that is not ours.

We are not, of course, foolish enough to imagine that we ought to find in ourselves the absolute omnipotence of God. Yet in our desire to be "as gods"—a lasting deformity impressed in our nature by original sin—we seek what one might call a relative omnipotence: the power to have everything we want, to enjoy everything we desire, to demand that all our wishes be satisfied and that our will should never be frustrated or opposed. It is the need to have everyone else bow to our judgment and accept our declarations as law. It is the insatiable thirst for recognition of the excellence which we so desperately need to find in ourselves to avoid despair. This claim to omnipotence, our deepest secret and our inmost shame, is in fact the source of all our sorrows, all our unhappiness, all our dissatisfactions, all our mistakes and deceptions. It is a radical falsity which rots our moral life in its very roots because it makes everything we do more or less a lie. Only the thoughts and actions which are free from the contamination of this secret claim have any truth or nobility or value in them.

This radical psychological claim to omnipotence is the deep impurity which stains and divides the pure soul of man. This demand, on the part of a limited being, to be treated as the Absolute and Supreme Being is the terrible illusion which dooms us to the slavery of passion, and of madness, and of sin.

Obviously, only the psychotic are able to come right out and state this hidden claim in the open. And that is what makes them psychotic. They have given up the relative sanity which demands that we keep this absurd fantasy hidden in the depths of our souls. They have asserted a right to disregard reality altogether and to live in a world that fits their own imagined ideal: that is to say, they have come out openly as "god" by calling into being a universe of their own making and annihilating (as far as they can do so) all other reality.

Those whom we agree, among ourselves, to call "sane" are those who keep their personal claim to absolute perfection and omnipotence repressed and disguised under certain accepted mental symbols, and who only assert their claim in actions which are rendered acceptable by an apparent outward harmlessness and social utility.

There are many acceptable and "sane" ways of indulging one's illusory claim to divine power. One can be, for example, a proud and tyrannical parent—or a tearful and demanding martyr-parent. One can be a sadistic and overbearing boss, or a nagging perfectionist. One can be a clown, or a dare-devil, or a libertine. One can be rigidly conventional, or blatantly unconventional; one can be a hermit or a demagogue. Some satisfy their desire for divinity by knowing everybody else's business: others by judging their neighbor, or telling him what to do. One can even, alas, seek sanctity and religious perfection as an unconscious satisfaction of this deep, and hidden impurity of soul which is man's pride.

The great enemy of monastic purity of heart is, then, the basic hidden project to be better than everybody else, to assert one's own freedom at the expense of every other freedom, to exalt one's own will over the wills of others, and to elevate one's own spirit above the spirits of lesser men.

From this basic, central project, come all other projects and illusory ideals. The impure soul is devoured and divided by its own incessant efforts to assert its radical claim while keeping that claim disguised under an acceptable exterior.

The life of a pure soul becomes exceedingly simple. But the impure soul is, and must be, most complicated. There are so many things to be done! One must assert himself, and exalt himself, and at the same time think himself self-sacrificing and humble. One must cherish, at all costs, the feeling of holiness and nobility on which one's peace and happiness depend. One must therefore be quick to note all the weaknesses and imperfections of other men, because they are potential rivals. And one must take care to see that these others are "charitably" punished and "sweetly" humiliated, lest they raise their heads as high as ours on the royal road to sanctity. One must take care that, while he openly "renounces" his own will, his will is secretly satisfied. One must make sure that no desire goes unfulfilled. In a word, one's own will must be done on earth as God's will is done in heaven!

Since all this is manifestly impossible, St Bernard points out that such a soul is inevitably subject to insecurity and fear. And fear is the "color" which darkens the soul and obscures the divine image, distorting it into an idol and a caricature. Fear is the "impurity" of the soul that aspires to be omnipotent.

Fallen man, then, is one in whom the Divine Image, or free-will, has become a slave to itself by making itself its own idol. The image of God is distorted by "unlikeness." Under the tyranny of such an idol, freedom itself becomes a kind of slavery, in which man drives himself wild trying to will what is impossible, trying to verify and prove his impossible claim to be a "god."

What is the answer? We have already seen it. It is the sacrament of the Cross, the faith and obedience of Christ which, as St Peter says, purify our hearts.* The interior pride of fallen man must be crucified on the Cross of Truth. Love of Truth and of the Cross overturns the idol, reduces man to his real level, restores to him his freedom, delivers him from fear, strengthens him in charity and enables him to live and act as a son of God. "For the truth shall make you free" (John, 8:32).

And so St Benedict, after describing the twelve steps of interior and exterior humility (each one of which is a participation in the mys-

* *Castificantes corda vestra in obedientia caritatis* (I Peter, 1:22).

tery of the obedience of Christ) declares that "when all these steps have been climbed the monk will at once reach that perfect charity which casts out fear." *

Purity of heart, perfect love, is the beginning of unity within the monk himself. Delivered from illusions and selfish projects, saved from the painful necessity to serve his own inexorable will, the monk begins to see how sweet is the yoke of Christ's service and how light is the burden of divine liberty! His eyes are open, and he begins for the first time to see himself, and other men as they are. No longer bound to satisfy his own whims and appetites first of all, he finds that all things bring him joy and happiness because he tastes them in the freedom of the sons of God. That is to say he can use them without belonging to them, and have them without being their slave.

Purity of heart, too, is the beginning of the monk's union with his brothers. His true union: for monastic charity is not merely a "social contract," a bargain arrived at by the agreement of many egoisms. It is the purity of heart which is reached only when all the separate wills of the brethren become one will, the common will, the will of Christ. This community of wills cannot be attained by a business-deal. It is an embrace of souls in the purity of the Spirit of God.

* Rule, c.7.

This embrace of united purities, of clean and disinterested wills, of souls lost in the light of God, is the highest point of the cenobitic ideal. All the souls called to union with God are fused together like iron in the fire and transformed together in the Light of God. Then God Himself lives and acts and manifests Himself in them. He knows Himself in them, embraces His own goodness in them by enabling them to share it with one another. As the Father is in the Son, so the Son is in them, and they are one with one another in the Father and the Son. This is the fulfillment of the Eucharistic mystery which is the heart of the monastic life.

But when will such fulfillment be realized? Can it be attained perfectly on this earth? Who can say? But in any case, when monks live together as they should, in the charity of Christ and the purity of the Spirit of God, bearing one another's burdens and helping one another to find themselves in Him, they are at least beginning on earth to build the heavenly city.

2. *In Veritate* [In Truth]

Everywhere in the Rules and writings of the Fathers, we hear the echoes of a word which resounds in the profoundest depths of the monastic heart: *veritas, verus, vere*. The word "truth" has been so abused that it has lost some of its impact on our minds. We are no longer fully alive to its value. The true is what is real, actual. It is true because it *is*. And that is what the monk is seeking: reality. He seeks that which *is*. Or rather, he seeks reality in Him Who is infinitely real, and truth in Him Who is True. But He does not seek truth merely as a concept, or as an object. He seeks the existential truth that is only found by entering into the mysterious actuality of life itself. He seeks the truth that is possessed when it is rightly lived, the reality that enters into the warp and woof of our own being if we make it our own by doing good—"faith which worketh by charity" (Galatians, 5:6).

A monk is one who lives "in truth"—*dans le*

vrai. His mission in life is to become so real, under the action of the Spirit of Him Who is, that his own life is a pure "amen," a conscious echo, freely replying "Yes" to the infinite reality and goodness of God.

Cistercian asceticism, and indeed all the asceticism of the monastic Fathers, is simply the recovery of our true self, man's true "nature," created for union with God. It is the purification, and liberation of the divine image in man, hidden under layers of "unlikeness." Our true self is the person we are meant to be—the man who is free and upright, in the image and likeness of God. The work of recovery of this lost likeness is effected by stripping away all that is alien and foreign to our true selves—shedding the "double garment" of hypocrisy and illusion by which we try to conceal the truth of our misery from ourselves, our brethren and from God.

If the monk is to build a solid and enduring temple to the glory of God—the monastic community united in perfect charity—he must first of all work at making himself real. He must discover the truth about himself. The foundation of the sacred edifice is the humility of all its living stones. Only by building on truth can we build solidly. And this means not only honesty but self-denial—the generous effort to sweep out of our lives all that is useless, all that is "alien" all that is not willed for us by God. Only then can we be our true selves.

William of St. Thierry says:

Man's work is constantly to prepare his heart by disengaging his will from alien desires, his reason from anxieties, and his memory from useless, and even some times from necessary cares. But a neglected will means useless thoughts; a corrupt will means perverse thoughts . . . while an upright will engages in the concerns that are necessary for this life. But a *loving* will begets thoughts that are capable of tasting the goodness of God.*

If we ask what the monastic Fathers consider to be "alien" to the soul of man, they tell us that material and created things, temporal values seen as ends in themselves, are foreign to us. For our souls are spirits, created for the highest of all spiritual and eternal goods. This is no manichaean or gnostic philosophy. It is not a crude division between matter and spirit that they envisage. They know well enough that that would only be to divide man against himself, since man is, in fact, constituted by body and soul together. It takes the perfect union of matter and spirit to make a true human person, and we do not increase our humanity or our sanctity by simply "delivering the spirit from the body."

---

* *Epistola ad Fratres de Monte Dei*, II, 14, Migne P.L. 184:347.

And so, in a certain sense, since we have bodies, bodily things are not alien to us. We are in our own connatural element, in the created world. What is alien to us in the *love* of material things. A man does not cease to be human merely because he is in the company of animals; he loses his humanity, he becomes alienated from himself, when his desires and values are those of an animal. And so, the soul that is enslaved by the need for sensible pleasure, or for self-assertion, or for material security has taken upon himself an "alien form," an unlikeness to his true self created in God's image.

Why dost thou impress upon thy soul a form that is not thine, indeed an alien deformity? For the things which thou delightest to have, thou fearest to lose: and fear is a color. As soon as it touches our liberty, it stains it and renders it unlike to itself.*

The whole purpose of the monastic life is to purify man's freedom from this "stain" of servility which it has contracted by its enslavement to things that are beneath it. Hence the true monk is one who is perfectly free. Free for what? Free to love God. Freedom, in the monastic context, does not imply the capacity to choose evil rather than good, but rather the capacity to prefer good

---

* St. Bernard, *Serm. 82 in Cantica*, n.4. P.L. 183: 1179.

over evil without ever being deluded by false appearances of good.

Hence St Bernard describes perfect freedom as: "being unable to will what is evil or to be without what is good." * He hastens to add that this perfection is only achieved in heaven, but admits that a foretaste of it can be attained in the present life. William of St Thierry echoes him, and adds an important note: that this supreme freedom comes from a perfect union of wills with God:

This unity of spirit makes man one with God not only by a union in which both will the same thing, but by a union in which our will is incapable of willing anything that is not willed by God— *aliud velle non valendi.***

The whole monastic life tends toward this summit of liberty, and it is in the light of this freedom of spirit that we must see and understand all the discipline of the monk, his austerities, his sacrifices, his rules, his obedience and his vows. The monk leaves the world with its false freedom, and by renouncing the weakness of will that drives him to obey every impulse and satisfy all his passions, he disciplines himself in obedience to the will of God, strengthens his soul in love, which brings him

---

* *De gratia et Libero Arbitrio*, c.6. n.20. P.L. 182:1012.
** *Epist. ad Fratres de Monte Dei*, II, n16, P.L. 184:349.

to a purer knowledge of God, unites himself more closely in pure charity with his brethren until his soul rests in that tranquil peace which is the sign that there are no longer any significant obstacles to frustrate his desire for truth. And where does he find this truth? In fulfilling the end for which his nature was created: that is to say in pleasing God by a love which responds to the free love of God with a love equally pure, and disinterested and free.

3. *In Laboribus Multis* [In Many Labors]

We find, in the Rule of St Benedict, that the monk does not treat material creation with contempt. On the contrary, we find the humblest material things handled with reverence, one might almost say with love. If the monk loves his monastery, it is because it is the "house of God and the gate of heaven" and he sees in it something of the beauty of heaven hidden among the trees of the forest. In a word, the humble stone buildings, the cloister set in the peaceful valley, the plain wooden furniture of the monastery, the bare little table and the trestle of planks in the monk's cell, far from being merely despised as "vain creatures" are respected and valued and even loved, not for their own sakes but for the sake of God to whom they belong. Even the tools with which the monk tills the soil, even the simple pots and pans and kitchenware, or the broom with which he sweeps the cloister, are to be treated with just as much care (within due proportion) as the sacred vessels of the altar (*Rule*, Chap. 31).

The love, the joy which we can and indeed must take in created things, depends entirely on our detachment. As soon as we take them to ourselves, appropriate them, hug them to our hearts, we have stolen them from God. They are no longer His, but our own. And then they are seen in a new light: they are seen in reference to ourselves, as if we were first cause and last end of their existence, as if they had to serve us the way all created things serve God, their Creator. But then we expect the impossible. Just as created things reflect the beauty and goodness of God, so we too avidly seek to find, in our friends and in the things we love, a reflection of our own superior excellence. But we are always disappointed. Our possessions give us the lie. Our friends evade our importunate expectations, embarrassed by the unseemly hunger of a pride which they know they can never satisfy, even though they allow themselves to be consumed by it.

Before a man can taste true joy in all the beautiful things that God has made, he must train the delicate interior sense which enables him to learn the lesson of wisdom which these modest creatures teach those who have ears to hear. They say to us: "You can use me, and God our Father created me that I might be used by you. I am His messenger, sent to tell you the way to Him. I contain a little of His goodness hidden in the depth of my being. But in order to perceive my goodness, you must respect my dignity as a creature of God. If you seek to deflower the pure integrity of my being, and take me to yourself as if I could be fully possessed by you, you will destroy me, and the beauty God has placed in me will vanish out of your hands. Then you will have profited in no way, you will lose me and defile your own soul. But if you respect me, and leave me as I am, and do not seek to seize me with a full and selfish possession, then I will bring you joy: for I will remain what I am, until by God's will I am changed by the service in which you use me. But in being thus changed I will not be destroyed, for use is not destruction. If you use me, my goodness is taken up to the level of your spirit. By using me in your service of God you consecrate me to Him along with yourself. And thus both of us, who were good from the first as creatures of God, help one another to become holy in Him."

This explains why some monastic buildings, and the things which are made and used there, are so beautiful. The purity of taste in a monastery is not merely a matter of aesthetic training. It flows from something far higher—from purity of heart. The simple, chaste lines of a monastic Church, built perhaps by unskilled hands in the wilderness, may well say infinitely more in praise of God than the pretentious enormities of costly splendor that are erected to be looked at rather than to be prayed in.

Monks are not always, or even usually, famous artists. It is indeed within the scope of their vocation for them to study and practice the various arts. But the value of their creations will always lie deeper in the spirit than can be explained by a "virtue of the practical intellect." The art of the monk is the fruit of a tree whose roots are charity, and poverty, and prayer.

A phrase which Eric Gill loved to quote is nowhere more true than in a monastery: "The artist is not a special kind of man, but every man is a special kind of artist." *

Every monk is, or should be, a special kind of artist. Nothing is more alien to the monastic life

---

* Eric Gill, *Essays*, passim. The saying belongs originally to *Ananda Coomaraswamy*.

than the cult of art for art's sake. The monk ought never to be an aesthete, but rather a "workman," a "craftsman"—*artifex*. Of course, St Benedict by no means supposed that all the monks were craftsmen: but all ought to be able to do useful and productive work. If the work consists in making something, so much the better.

As soon as we see that monastic work is supposed to be productive, or even creative, we understand immediately that work is more than just a penitential exercise for the monk. Manual labor is quite often hard labor, and rightly so. If man has been endowed with muscles by God, it is proper that he use them. Laborious work in the fields and forests, ploughing, splitting logs, breaking rock, harvesting: these all contribute much to a healthy and well-integrated spiritual life. And when the work is difficult or servile, the self-denial it demands is an admirably effective penance. But it should always be more than a mere "penitential exercise"—a term which would seem to suggest that the work had no other purpose than penance.

An overemphasis on the "painful" aspect of labor tends to make one forget that good work requires discipline of the practical intelligence. The monk must not only grit his teeth and accept the necessity of sweating more than he would ordinarily like. He must also be able to think, to work wisely and well, to direct his efforts to the accomplishment of what needs to be done. He is not only expiating his own private sins, he is working for the support of his brothers and for the poor.

"Doing" things, "making" things are indeed activities: but not all activity is excluded, by its very nature, from a life of contemplation. This truth is as old as the desert Fathers. St Anthony, we are told, was taught by an angel wisely to alternate work and prayer, and the desert Fathers were famous for the weaving of baskets as well as for the exercize of many other more intricate skills, including even the practice of medicine.

Where we find buildings that are ugly, furniture ill-made, doors that do not close properly, vines and fruit trees clumsily pruned, materials and fodder going to waste, the lack of skill and care which these things represent might simply be the fruit of a wrong attitude toward work itself a false orientation of the monastic spirit.

No useful work that can be carried on within the enclosure is foreign to the monastic state. Most monks might be expected to have their fair share of digging in the garden, pitching hay, chopping wood, peeling potatoes, washing dishes and sweeping floors. All the ordinary tasks of a community living in the country might rightly claim the time of the community members.

Some of the monks will be almost exclusively employed at the "common work." Others will have special jobs assigned to them—anything from cheese-making to bee-keeping, from carpentry to the writing of books, from baking bread to painting a fresco. Someone will have to do the cooking. In the old days each monk took his turn at cooking the dinner for one week, but now it has been found more practical as well as more merciful to make this important office a more permanent appointment. When buildings are going up, there will doubtless be a monastic architect drawing up the plans, and the monks will provide most of the labor, with a little expert help from an outside contractor. There will have to be bakers, and shoe-makers, and tailors. There may be weavers, bookbinders, tanners. Modern life lays a rather heavy burden of work on the monastery plumber, and electrician, not to mention the garage mechanic.

Intellectual work has always held a place of honor in monasteries, though it is less emphasized by some Orders than by others. Scholarship as such is by no means out of place in the cloister, although when it involves too much travelling and too heavy a correspondence it tends to interfere with the peace of monastic solitude. Teaching, on a small scale, is provided for in the Rule of St Benedict and even a certain restricted ministry may be expected, but since the demands in these spheres are so apt to increase in geometrical progression, monks are wisely reluctant to take on the responsibility for a task which is not properly their own. For teaching and preaching though they may perhaps occasionally be allowed an accidental place in the framework of a monastic vocation, can never be allowed to become the immediate end of that vocation. The monastic life has its end only in God. It cannot be systematically diverted to any other finality. A monastic community may maintain a school, but it may never exist *for the sake of* the school which it maintains.

We must always remember that silence, solitude, recollection and prayer are the most important elements in the monastic life. They are the most direct aids to that charity which unites the monk to God and his brethren. If, in a certain sense, silence and contemplation can be said to exist "for the sake of" the apostolate in the mendicant Orders (although even with them this statement would be erroneous and misleading) they cannot be said to serve any other purpose, for the monk, than to favor his own union with God and, thereby, his fruitfulness as a holy member of the Communion of saints. Everything in the monastery, then, is

33

ordered to produce the atmosphere propitious for a life of prayer. The isolation of the monastery itself, the work by which the monks strive to be self-supporting and independent of secular contacts, the reading and study which are done in the cloister or in the cell, and the office chanted in choir all have for their function to keep the monastery what it is meant to be: a sanctuary where God is found and known, adored and in a certain way "seen" in the darkness of contemplation.

4. *In Tabernaculo Altissimi*

The monastery is a tabernacle in the desert, upon which the *shekinah*, the luminous cloud of the divine Presence, almost visibly descends. The monk is one who lives "in the secret of God's face," immersed in the divine presence. Just as the children of Israel, at the command of God, speaking through Moses, contributed materials and labor with which the skilled workmen constructed the tabernacle of the Testament, so the monastic community, guided by the Abbot and Father, who speaks as the representative of God, pools all its goods and efforts in the work of constructing a sanctuary. The monastery is never merely a house, a dwelling for men. It is a Church, a sanctuary of God. It is a Tabernacle of the New Testament, where God comes to dwell with men not merely in a miraculous cloud but in the mystical humanity of His divine Son, Whom the cloud prefigured.

The monks, working together with a spirit of self-sacrifice and perfect solidarity, are not merely providing for their material needs in this life. Their work also contributes to a much more important common spiritual end: their union in Christ. Building and maintaining the monastery, they are building the new Jerusalem, a little mystical Body of Christ, the "Church" of their monastery. For the building of stones in which they chant the office is merely the outward symbol and expression of the building of living stones which is formed by the monks themselves. As St Bernard told the monks of Clairvaux on the feast of the Dedication of their Church:

Be not like horses and mules which have no understanding. What sanctity can these stones have, that we should celebrate their feast? Yet they are indeed holy, but because of your bodies . . . Holy are your souls because the Holy Spirit dwells in them; holy are your bodies because of your souls; and holy is this house because of your bodies.*

Now the members of the monastic community build this spiritual temple, of which they themselves form the stones, by their charity. This charity consists not merely in the labor of bearing one another's burdens, of supporting one another in their pilgrimage towards the heavenly Jerusalem. It consists of something far more than corporal works of mercy, good example, instruction and the rest. The monastic community exists not merely in order that each individual may find support, exhortation, correction and encouragement, but also and above all that all may more easily attain to their common end, which is union with God in solitude.

The monks therefore help one another not only to grow grain and produce the bread of the body, but also bring one another to the spiritual ovens of solitude from which they are nourished with the hot, fresh bread of the Spirit. They not only press the grapes of their vineyards into material wine, but they lead one another to the eternal fountains of silence in which they drink the living waters and the rich wine of the Holy Spirit.

But even this spiritual refection of the monks themselves is not the most important thing in

---

* *Serm. 1 in Dedicatione Eccles.*, n.1, P.L. 183:518.

the monastery. What is far more important still is that the Word of God comes silently into their midst, and eats and drinks with them, Divine Wisdom not only gives them wine to drink, but "takes His delight with the children of men."

It is because the monks enable one another to live most easily and peacefully in solitude and silence, because they provide for one another an atmosphere of recollection and solitude and prayer, that they are able to achieve the supreme end of the monastic life which is this spiritual and hidden banquet—the feast in which the Word sits down at table with His chosen ones and finds pleasure and consolation in their company. And He says: "I have come into my garden . . . I have eaten the honeycomb with my honey: I have drunk my wine with my milk: eat, O friends, and drink: be inebriated, O my dearly beloved" (Canticle 5:1).

This is the true, essential and perfect meaning of the common life. The monastery is a "Tabernacle of the Testament" or, if you prefer, another Cenacle in which Jesus sits down at table with His disciples, nourishing them with His own substance which is the very Wisdom and Glory of God. The monastery is first and above all a *tabernaculum Dei cum hominibus*, a "gate of heaven," a place where God comes down in His infinite charity to let Himself be seen and known by men. Everything vital and fruitful in the monastery derives its vitality from the fact that it contributes to this one essential end.

The silence of the forest, the peace of the early morning wind moving the branches of the trees, the solitude and isolation of the house of God: these are good because it is in silence, and not in commotion, in solitude and not in crowds, that God best likes to reveal Himself most intimately to men. The humble work in the fields, the labor in the shops, kitchens and bakeries, is good because it divides and disperses the burdens of material life, distributes the cares and responsibilities so that no one monk has too many material things to think about. Each one contributes his share in peace and recollection, without undue anxiety. No one has to worry for the morrow, and the monk, as Cassian long ago pointed out, is able to live in all its perfection the Gospel counsel to "Take no thought for the morrow," and to "seek first the kingdom of God and His justice" (Matthew, 7:33-34). In the common chanted psalmody in choir, the *opus Dei* is meant to be made not burdensome but light and easy. The very fact of chanting the psalms together enhances their meaning of those great prophecies which are fulfilled today in the Mystical Christ, of Whom the monk is an articulate and fully conscious member.

In the common regular places of the monastery the silence and recollection with which the monks work, study and pray together enhances the whole atmosphere of silent work and prayer. The union of all these souls in a common effort, a common silence, and a single-minded charity makes the fruit of each one's prayers, merits and virtues become the spiritual possession of all.

The monk who feels himself to be most destitute in virtue and in grace can be rich in both if he has the humility and charity to share the virtues of his brothers by rejoicing in them as if they were his own. And the strongest and most virtuous of all become stronger still by the humility which makes them realize that their virtues are not due to their own efforts alone but to the prayers and encouragement of their brothers. Nor should this manner of speaking induce us to imagine that the true monk wastes time comparing himself with his brother in this matter of virtue and of grace. On the contrary, his charity makes him realize the futility of such a thought.

The true goods of the spiritual life are those which are not diminished by being shared but which, on the contrary, are possessed all the more perfectly when they are shared with others. The common faith of the monastic body is daily increased by the celebration of Mass and the chanting of the office in common. The same liturgical life, and the common patience with which the community sustains its tribulations, increases the hope of each one while enhancing the hope of the whole body. And the greatest of all the virtues, charity, which includes all the others and embraces so to speak the whole monastic life within its compass, grows in all with each vital spiritual act of each member of the community.

This theology of the common life is, paradoxically, the justification for the presence of solitaries in the monastic body. The solitary vocation is rare today, but that does not mean that it does not exist at all, still less that it has no longer any reason for existing. The Camaldolese hermit may have greater solitude and austerity by becoming a recluse, dwelling alone and unvisited in his hermitage. It is quite logical that one member or another of a Benedictine or Cistercian community be allowed by his abbot, after a careful testing of his vocation, to separate himself in some measure from the rest to devote himself more fully to prayer. He may be less visibly engaged in the exterior manifestations of the common life, but if he fulfills his function well and becomes a more fruitful agent in the common life, he enters, as it were, into the spiritual heart of the common life by attaining more perfectly to the common end for which the whole community is striving. In doing so, he helps all the others to achieve the same end by following the ordinary way which is the vocation and the preference of the majority.

Whatever may be the individual monk's place in the monastic community, whether he be a man of active temperament whose spirituality expresses itself in works of mercy, or whether he be a superior, helping the Abbot in the work of running the monastery, or a father entrusted with the guidance and formation of souls, or a contemplative and solitary spirit, each one contributes to the common life of the whole body by fulfilling his own peculiar function in it.

The important thing is for each one to realize that his life and value as a member of a spiritual organism depends on the clearsighted freedom and generous self-dedication with which he co-operates with the other members under their Abbot in working for their common end. This demands more than a mere intellectual assent to an abstract proposition. It means breaking down that interior resistance and coldness of heart which ascetic terminology calls "self-will." Self-will is simply the determination to seek our own private good in preference to a good that is common to ourselves and others. Now a good that is shared with others, is, as we

have seen, higher and more spiritual, and therefore more perfect, than one which we can only
enjoy by the exclusion of some others or of all.
Self-will is therefore an "exclusive" will, which
pushes others out of our life in order to enjoy
values that are too small to be shared with more
than a few, or even with anyone at all. Self-
will is inseparable from fear, anxiety, and spiritual slavery. The mechanism of the common life,
which constantly breaks in upon the privacy
and exclusiveness of our own self-will, is ex-
pressly designed to break down the resistance
with which we prevent our full spiritual in-
corporation in the social life of the monastery.
Yet at the same time the common life is never
intended to deprive a man of his true interior
liberty, or to encroach upon his own personality, still less to break and destroy these highest
of values. For if self-will narrows us down and
encloses us within a privacy that is too small to
permit real growth of interior freedom, it is
clear that unselfish devotion to a common cause
is one of the ways in which our freedom and
personal autonomy are best able to develop and
to mature.

It would therefore be a perversion of monastic doctrine to imagine that the common life is
designed merely to "break" man's will and to
dissolve his personality in a formless mass without any individual character at all. There is all

the difference in the world between a community and a crowd. A community is an organism whose common life is pitched on a somewhat higher tone than the life of the individual member. A crowd is a mere aggregation in which the collective life is as low as the standards of the lowest units in the aggregation. In entering a community, the individual sets himself the task of living above his own ordinary level, and thus perfecting his own being, living more fully, by his efforts to live for the benefit of others besides himself. Descending into the crowd, the individual loses his personality and his character and perhaps even his moral dignity as a human being. Contempt for the "crowd" is by no means contempt for mankind. The crowd is below man. The crowd devours the human that is in us to make us the members of a many-headed beast. That is why the monastery builds itself in the wilderness: cuts off communications with the world, and with the press and the radio which too often are simply the voice of the vast aggregation that is something less than human. As a specialized, spiritual society, the monastic community must take care to form itself carefully in the atmosphere of solitude and detachment in which the seeds of faith and charity have a chance to sink deep roots and grow without being choked out by thorns, or crushed under the wheels of trucks and cars.

St Paul, in describing the pagan world which has lost the knowledge of God through its own fault, lists many of the sins which make that world truly pagan: "Filled with all iniquity, malice, immorality, avarice . . . full of envy, murder, contention, deceit, malignity . . . being detractors . . . irreverent, proud, haughty" (Romans, 1:29-30). As usual in these lists of vices, we find that the listed sins are polarized around one central point: a hard-hearted selfishness which is turned away from the common good and from God and centered on a private and exclusive good that has to be defended against the whole universe and which, in the end, has to be lost because it is only an illusion. Ending this particular list which we have quoted, Paul adds the following climax. It is significant that these evil qualities sound to us trifling and mild. The pagan world is, he says, "foolish, dissolute, without affection, without fidelity, without mercy" (Romans, 1:31).

The monastery builds itself in solitude in order that the monastic community may become the exact opposite of all that has been listed here. The fruit of the spirit is harvested in silence and isolation—"charity, joy, peace, patience, kindness, goodness, faith, modesty, continency" (Galatians, 5:22-23).

The common life of the monastery by its simplicity and poverty sobers us and delivers us from the frivolous spirit of a world that laughs at everything. The austerity and hard work pull us together and strengthen the sinews of our will to resist the dissoluteness with which the worldly man and his society are always falling apart. But it is above all important to realize that the monastic life is a school of affection, fidelity and mercy. By sharing the prayers, labors and trials of our brothers, and knowing them as they are, we learn to respect them and to love them with a sober compassion that is too deep for sentimentality. We learn to be faithful to them, depending on them, we know that they have a right to depend on us. We try to learn how not to fail them. Finally we forgive others their faults and sins against us, as we ourselves would be forgiven by them and by God. In this school of charity and of peace a man learns not only to respect and to love others, but also, in the purest sense, to love and respect his own person for the sake of God. Without this supernatural self-respect, which comes from realizing himself to be sincerely loved by another, man can hardly find it in himself to have true affection for his brothers. This deep mutual respect is nourished in the monastery. It is the exact opposite to worldly flattery because it is based on a true and intimate knowledge of others and of ourselves. Its fruit is a solid and lasting peace which does not end with the mere satisfaction of our

45

natural need for companionship and for friends, but purifies our hearts of dependence on visible things and strengthens our faith in God. For, in the last analysis, the warmth of monastic charity is the warmth not of nature alone but of the unseen and infinite fire which burns in the hidden depths of the Blessed Trinity.

These men do not live by their own spirit, but by the Spirit of God who leads them and makes them sons of God, and who is the love and the bond which unites them. And the greater is their love, the more firmly are they bound together and the fuller is their communion. Inversely, the greater their communion, the more firmly are they united and the fuller is their love. I now speak of that love by which we are to love God before all and above all. And this love is what gives form to every good life, in order to make it good.*

Obviously, everything in the monastic society is not always consoling and perfect. Characters there are often as unpolished as anywhere else, and circumstances sometimes contribute to exaggerate the smallest difficulties and make them seem very great. But the fact remains that the objective character of the monastic life makes it a communion of brotherly affection in which not only the deep charity of the will is brought into play, but also the noblest and purest feel-

---

* Baldwin of Canterbury, *De Vita Coenobitica*, P.L. 204, 553.

ings of the human heart. The nobility of these
feelings is proportionate to their sincerity, and
their sincerity in turn is purified and without
illusion. The monastic body is held together not
by human admirations and enthusiasms which
make men heroes and saints before their time
but on the sober truth which accepts men exactly as they are in order to help them become
what they ought to be.

5. *In Unitate* [In Unity]

Watching over the destinies of this whole
body is the most important man in the monastery, the head on whom the action and peace
of the members must depend. He is the Abbot,
who, by his charismatic vocation holds the place
of Christ in the community. In using the term
charismatic here I do not intend to minimize the
hierarchical and juridical aspects of the abbatial
office, but only to emphasize the forgotten fact
that the man chosen to rule a community is also
chosen above all to sanctify its members and
therefore he is chosen because of his superior

47

holiness and knowledge of the things of God, his ability to discern and test the spirits of his followers and to guide his community in the light of divine counsel.

The abbot is the superior, a man of God who has been especially endowed with graces and gifts for the sake of the community. As the representative of God, he not only exercises a divinely given authority to rule, but is as it were a "sacrament" of the Fatherhood of God. He has a divine mission. He is "sent" to the community by Christ as Christ was sent into the world by the Father. Christ and the Father are therefore hidden in his person, speak in his words and will what he commands. He is sent to govern and to teach and to sanctify. All these powers are given him to be used in the line of God's providence for the souls and for the community entrusted to him. Therefore he must first of all understand what God's Providence is, since he is its instrument. This does not mean a magic ability to guess right and make cunning decisions by means of some kind of divination. It means knowledge of the Law of God, for the Abbot is *doctus lege divina*. It means understanding God's ordinary ways with men, the law of Christ, the law of charity. It means therefore understanding that just as God exercises his creative and sanctifying power for the good of the creatures He cherishes, so authority is given not in order to crush and subject human wills, but in order to form and develop them.

Not without reason did Christ say: "The Kings of the gentiles lord it over them, and they who exercise authority over them are called benefactors. But not so with you. On the contrary, let him who is the chief among you become as the servant" (Luke, 22:25-26).

The worldly prince is "called a benefactor" as though the benefits which he allows his subjects were a gift of his own largesse, rather than a right due to them. In the Christian dispensation the Apostle is one who comes to bring men the supernatural benefits and privileges which God wills them to have. In a sense he restores to them the peace, the nobility, the love, the strength which were originally intended for man's spirit, which were lost in the fall and recovered in the victory of Christ. The Abbot, therefore, should know well that his function is not arbitrarily to restrict and break the spiritual freedom of his sons, and make them subject to authority for authority's sake. He is on the contrary the one appointed by God to see that the gift of divine freedom and wisdom develops in their souls. If he is sometimes severe, his severity itself is intended to make them strong.

The Apostle Paul was impatient with the Corinthians not because they resisted his authority, but on the contrary precisely because some of them wanted to form a faction around him and exalt his authority above that of the other apostles (I Corinthians, 1:12-13). He saw that this obsession with human hero-worship and this desire for submission to a human leader was "childishness" in the spiritual order (*id*. 3:1). His mission was precisely to deliver them from this servile self-subjection to human traditions, human authority, human leadership, in order that they might develop their god-given freedom and live "in the Spirit" as mature Christians.

It is the function of the Abbot in the monastery to lead his sons to this spiritual maturity which is Christian liberty and wisdom. For this he must be mature and wise and free himself. Then he will be able to raise up sons worthy to help him in his task, and one among them wise enough to replace him. The word wisdom therefore occurs very frequently in the pages of St Benedict. For him, the monk was assuredly not a grown up baby, incapable of managing himself or doing anything. The Benedictine has the true spiritual childhood of a soul which is mature because it is guided by the Holy Spirit. Only under such conditions is the house of God ruled wisely, as Benedict would have it to be, by wise men: *domus Dei a sapientibus sapienter administretur*.

The feasts of the liturgical year bring home

this mystery in a vivid and symbolic manner. The monastic family gathers with a special solemnity in the abbatial Church. There, before the high altar, the community takes special cognizance of its supernatural character and vocation. With a touch of splendor not out of keeping with the sobriety of the monastic state, the Abbot assumes his mitre and crozier and the pontifical vestments and goes up to celebrate the sacred mysteries surrounded by his sons, ministering to him in various capacities. Here the whole community is one in its great work of "being" another Christ, of offering with Christ, the Church's sacrifice of praise and adoration. In order that this sacrifice may be true and acceptable to God, it must proceed from a unified and integrated mystical organism in which Christ Himself lives and acts by His Holy Spirit. Such an organism is symbolized by the solemn Pontifical ceremonies in which the Abbot, as Head, and representative of Christ, allows himself to be assisted at the altar by his priests and deacons. The older, more mature men, who have received the honor of sacred Orders, stand by the Abbot's side as he offers the Holy Sacrifice. The younger ones take their turn in singing the liturgical texts and bringing to the altar the matter for sacrifice. Another young monk offers the sacred incense. The youngest, still new in the liturgical life, also have their share, one holding the candle, another the book, others the Abbot's crozier and mitre. Then the whole body of the monastic choir accompanies the Mass with solemn chants.

Everything here speaks of Christ living in His Church, Christ the High Priest of all Creation, the Word in Whom all things subsist, the Lamb slain from the beginning of the world. But above all everything speaks eloquently of the "monastic Christ," the mystical body of members united with their head, in close solidarity and zealous fraternal love, living out their lives as a sacrifice of praise in honor of the eternal Father.

The unity symbolized here is not only the juridical unity of a body of members submissive to the authority of their head, but also the spiritual unity of a mystical organism which outwardly manifests the interior and hidden reality of the Communion of Saints.

When the Abbot celebrates pontifical Mass at the altar, we see present not only the monastic body unified in one heart and one voice in prayer, but the whole Mystical Body of Christ, united with Christ in His adoration of the Father. And we remember that the invisible reality is far greater than the one we see. We understand once again the tremendous hiddenness and silence which underly the words and thoughts and symbols of our faith.

Here, we are in presence of the invisible and perfect liturgy of heaven, a liturgy incomprehensible to our minds, whose songs are silent, whose prayers are hidden in God—a liturgy of praise that goes forth from God like a river of fire to burn in His creatures and draw them into His hidden glory, sending them forth again enriched with a life that must ever increase by plunging back into the vast sea of Being which encompasses all.

Here, before the altar, where the community gathers for the Eucharistic banquet, we know that the solitaries of the desert are also present. This is their Mass as well as ours. We know that the captives and confessors of the faith, hidden in the jails and mines of the persecutor, are also present. This is their Mass perhaps even more than ours. We know that the souls buried in the mystery of death, and not yet purified, are present. It is their Mass as well as ours. We remember finally that the whole body of Monasticism, past, present and to come, is there in a special way, and that the entire Church is present for it is her sacrifice. And the whole Church of God is one in charity and in the Spirit of Jesus Christ. This charity, poured forth by the Holy Spirit, is the life and form and activating principle of monasticism: it is hidden, silent, buried in mystery. But there is also a visible element, a

53

material factor, which must be animated by this hidden Spirit.

The material element, the flesh and bone, which invest this solitary spirit with a power to act in the world of men, is to be sought in monastic observance. Observance varies in its details from one family to another, but in its essentials it is always the same. It sets up a framework within which the main duties of the monk are carried out. In our time in which few monks actually live in the desert, the rules and usages of the monastery create something of a spiritual desert of silence, solitude, detachment, poverty, austerity, labor and prayer.

Variations in monastic discipline depend largely on how far each different rule seeks to accommodate itself to the limitations of the human subject. The best monastic rules are not necessarily the most austere, for strictness is not the only norm of value in the monastery. Those rules are best which are best adapted to their end —helping men of flesh and blood effectively to lead lives of prayer. If the rule is too austere, the monk may become a machine for doing penance, but he will cease to be a man of prayer. More often than not, the rule will break him instead of making him into what he ought to be. If the rule is not austere enough, the monk will let himself get too soft for prayer and spiritual discipline, and will become, in fact, a comfortable (though perhaps anxious) citizen—another inert member of the middle class.

The most austere rules, and those which seek to reproduce as closely as possible the original purity of the monastic life, place more emphasis on solitude, penance, silence, manual labor, contemplative prayer. The less austere rules while retaining a definite realization that the monk is a man of the desert, nevertheless turn in some degree toward the world, in order to provide a monastic life for the majority of vocations who would find the pure ideal unbearable. In these rules, greater emphasis is placed upon vocal and liturgical prayer, on works of mercy, community life, intellectual work, teaching and even the apostolic ministry.

These two tendencies, the one solitary and the other social, always unite together in every form of organized monasticism. Each monastery maintains, in some degree or other, a blend of the solitary life and the common life.

Carthusian monks lead a semi-eremitical life. Each monk has his own cell which, if one may so speak, forms part of a community of cells. The Camaldolese, who are perhaps the most flexible as well as the most traditional of all western monks in their observance, maintain both cenobitic and eremitical communities. A Camaldolese may be either a cenobite, or a hermit, or even a recluse. Thus in one form of life many different degrees of solitude can be found, up to and including one of the most absolute and most perfect.

The Trappist-Cistercians and certain Benedictine families like La Pierre qui Vire, maintain a truly cenobitical life in which solitude is guaranteed by the strict practice of silence and enclosure. La Pierre qui Vire is also a true representative of the Benedictine tradition which allows a hermitage within reach of the monastery and assumes that the Abbot will have sufficient discretion to tell which of his monks might be qualified to make good use of it.

The Benedictines of Solesmes, maintaining the principle of solitude and isolation from the world, and keeping silence within the monastery, are nevertheless conscious of a special mission, inherited from Cluny and St Maur, to present to the world the witness of a monastic Body fully aware of the presence and the glory of God. The liturgy and sacred scholarship then occupy the most important place in a community that is almost visibly the court of the King of Heaven.

The Cistercians of the Common Observance and some of the other great Benedictine Congregations, while clinging to scholarship and the liturgy, have served the Church in works of the apostolate, in preaching and teaching, without losing their essential orientation towards God in solitude.

The austere tradition of silent and contemplative monasticism is not without its elements of deep and vital humanism, but it is above all a tradition of detachment, austerity, faith and prayer. Study, liturgy, art, agriculture, education, and writing fit into the cadre of monastic austerity and solitude. Their place is, and must always be, secondary.

II

THE CENOBITIC LIFE

1. *St Benedict*

We have seen something of the monastic spirit. Now let us turn to the various forms in which this spirit takes flesh, for the monastic life is not simply disembodied spirit. It is incarnate in different kinds of observance which express different interpretations of the Benedictine Rule.

In its basic essentials, the monastic spirit is one and the same in all the various branches of the monastic Order. The accidental variations that distinguish the Cistercian from the monk of Solesmes, or the White Benedictine of Prinknash from the Camaldolese hermit are profound enough to constitute specific differences in their spirituality. All seek to glorify God and save their souls by a contemplative life, according to the Rule of St Benedict and guided by his spirit. Variations in observance depend largely on how far each monastic family stresses some one particular aspect of the Benedictine rule. But these particular applications of the Benedictine formula, while they *adapt* the essence of the Rule to certain special times, places and circumstances, may never permit themselves to change the essence of the monastic life itself.

Some Benedictine families lay stress on the austerity of the Rule, others are more open to its spirit of humanism and of discretion. Some affirm the essentially contemplative and solitary nature of the monastic ideal, others recall the fact that in practice St Benedict himself and the earliest Benedictines allowed the apostolate a definite place in the life of the monk. But in fact, these two tendencies, the one solitary and austere, the other social and humanistic, should always blend to some extent in all monastic life. The different proportions in which they are blended together will depend on the particular aim of each observance. And this particular aim will never be anything but a special way of arriving at the one end which Benedict has proposed for all his sons.

The monk is always and essentially a man of prayer and penance. His horizons are always and essentially those of the desert. He has left all things to deny himself and follow Christ in poverty, labor, humility. In a word, the monastic life is the Cross of Christ. If science, art, literature, education, historical research, and the apostolic ministry enter into this life, they do so only in so far as they can ultimately be fitted into this perspective that opens out upon the wilderness through which the monk must make his journey to God. If some interpretations of the Rule are less austere than others, it is because they hope to enable the average man to live as a contemplative without prejudice to his mental or physical health. If some monasteries wisely concern themselves with research in Scripture, the Fathers, liturgy and the chant, it is because they know that this is the most effective way by which a certain type of soul can nourish a life of prayer. The variations in monastic observances are all good and all necessary, in so far as they make the monastic life accessible to all types of men. He who is not able to qualify for one family will very likely find a place for himself in one of the others.

In spite of their differences, then, all the Benedictine families have something in common. Before considering their differences, let us see how they are one.

They have a common Father and a common Rule. The purpose of the Rule is to form Christ in the soul of the monk in much the same way as He was formed in the soul of St Benedict. The Rule, which is nothing more or less than Benedict's own way of life, shows us the particular manner in which a monk interprets and applies the lessons of the Gospel of Christ. A Benedictine monk is simply a man who understands the Gospel and lives it as it was understood and lived by St Benedict.

Who was St Benedict? How did he interpret the Gospel and apply it to his own life?

History tells us not so much what Benedict did as who he was. Most of the dates in his life are open to discussion. It is sufficient for us to place him in his century—the sixth. He was a Roman, who established the monastic life on a firm foundation in Italy, where it already existed, at the end of the great Barbarian invasions. His Rule, which was a summary of all the accumulated wisdom of eastern monasticism, eventually supplanted all other monastic rules in the west. Benedictine monasticism played such a tremendously important part in the reconstruction of Europe after the great migrations, that Benedict is rightly called not only the Father of western monasticism but simply the "Father of the West."

But now let us look at the living portrait which has been left of him by his biographer— St Gregory the Great—and by his own Rule. It is in the Rule and in the person of Benedict that we find the spirit, the "form" without which no monk can truly call himself a Benedictine.

The first trait that strikes us in the character

of St Benedict is his unusual seriousness. The Benedictine spirit is a spirit of maturity and depth. Even as a child, Benedict had the wisdom that is normally only gained by years of experience. Supernatural prudence gave him a piercing insight into the nothingness of worldly things, and he turned away from them to devote his life to God. His whole life is summed up in the words with which St Gregory describes him retiring to the lonely cave of Subiaco: "he sought to please God alone"—*soli Deo placere desiderans.*

Therefore his life was simple and austere. Putting aside everything that was not God, he lived alone under the eyes of God (*solus in superni spectatoris oculis habitavit secum*).* His life as a hermit was completely dependent upon Divine Providence, and indeed this faith in Providence was another of the great characteristics of Benedict who had decreed to give away (to the poor) all that he had on earth, in order that he might lay up treasures, for himself, in heaven.** In this, he followed the Gospel of Christ in all its literal simplicity. "Every one of you that doth not renounce all that he possesses, cannot be my disciple" (Luke, 14:33). "Sell what you

---

* "He dwelt alone, and by himself, under the eyes of Him who looks down from above." St Gregory, *Dialogues II*, P.L. 66, 136.
** Ibid, col. 186.

possess and give alms. Make to yourselves bags which grow not old, a treasure in heaven which faileth not: where no thief approacheth, and no moth corrupteth" (Luke, 12:33).

His life in the cave of Subiaco was a struggle for conquest of himself, of his passions, and of the evil spirits. Having at last attained to that *apatheia* (or freedom from passion) which qualified him to be a teacher * of other monks, Benedict found himself surrounded by the disciples who had been brought to him by the Holy Spirit, and his life as an Abbot and monastic founder began.

Persecuted by the hatred of envious men, he had a chance to practice in all its perfection the meekness with which Christ has commanded us to love our enemies.** Finally, amid all the cares of an abbot and of an apostle, he enjoyed the highest mystical contemplation, together with the charismatic gifts of prophecy miracles, the discernment of spirits. He was in the highest sense a "man of God," a man possessed and transfigured by the Holy Spirit, living and acting in the Spirit, seeing and knowing all things in the light of the Logos, so that at last he beheld all creation gathered together as it were "in a single ray of the sun." And St Gregory com-

---

* *Liber a tentationis vitio, jure jam factus est virtutum magister.* Ibid, col. 132.
** Ibid, col. 136.

ments: "To Him who sees the Creator, all creatures dwindle to nothingness." *

This then is the pattern from which the life
of each Benedictine monk must be cut. We
need not, indeed we cannot, reproduce in our
lives all the externals of St Benedict's life. Most
of us cannot live alone in caves—few of us will
ever enjoy his miraculous gifts. But we must be
men of God as he was; we must be transformed
by the Spirit of God as he was; we must abandon ourselves to the will of God as he did. We
must reproduce in ourselves the charity of Christ
as did Benedict. And we must long to see God
as he did.

How can this be done? The Rule gives us the
answer.

The essence of the Rule of St Benedict is the
renunciation of self-will in imitation of Christ
Who said: "I came not to do my own will, but
the will of Him Who sent me" (John, 6:38).
The Benedictine life is the following of Christ
in obedience, humility and charity. The monk
is another Christ, "obedient unto death." But
the purpose of this self-renunciation is not
merely to place us in subjection to a human superior. The vows and the Rule subject us to
God, teach us how to obey God. They aim to
place us under the direct guidance of the Divine

---

* Ibid, col. 260.

Spirit. When we are able to hear and understand and respond to each hidden impulsion of the Spirit, our lives are no longer dominated by fear. Then, as St Benedict says, we do all "for the love of Christ, and according to good habits and with delight in virtue—things which the Lord will deign to manifest, by His Holy Spirit, in the worker whom He has purified of vices and of sins." *

The life which St Benedict had in mind when he wrote the Rule was the life he himself was living when he wrote it. How did he live?

The monastery was a small simple building, or group of buildings, inhabited by a community of twelve or fifteen monks. One room was set aside as the oratory, there was another for the novices. St Benedict apparently had his own cell. There was a kitchen, a refectory, a common dormitory. Within the monastic enclosure were a mill, a bakery and various shops where the monks worked. The community was supported by the work of the monks themselves, and from time to time gifts might be brought by benefactors or left by rich travellers. St Benedict however was more interested in offering hospitality to the poor. But in any case, the monastery guest-house was a necessary part of the institution whose founder saw Christ in

* Rule, chapter 7, end.

every stranger, as well as in every member of his own monastic family.

The monks rose an hour or so after midnight to chant or recite a very simple office consisting of psalms and lessons, without any of the accretions and additions that have complicated the breviary since his day. Seven times in the day they assembled in the oratory or their place of work in the fields, to recite the canonical hours. Each of the "little hours" took about ten minutes to recite. The psalms were followed by a few moments of meditation in common, but St Benedict made a point of insisting that this should be short. The thing that most strikes us when we grasp the meaning of St Benedict's legislation for the monastic liturgy, is that he wants everything to be simple and brief, according to the words of Christ: "When you are praying speak not much as the heathens, for they think that in their much speaking they may be heard" (Matthew, 6:7). The Rule, however, leaves the individual monk free to prolong his prayer in private, according to the inspiration of the Holy Spirit.* In other words, the common, liturgical prayer should not become mere tedious routine, and private contemplative prayer is left to the free choice of each particular soul. In this way, St Benedict made

---

* Rule, chapter 20.

sure that when the monk carried out his principal obligation, the praise of God in choir, he would do so with a mind that was fresh and attentive to the words he recited.

The rest of the monk's day would then be divided between reading *(lectio divina)* and manual work. There might be anything from five to eight hours of work a day, with two or three hours of reading and meditation.

The meatless meals of the community were simple, but, compared with the diet of the desert Fathers, very plentiful, and there was ample time allowed for sleep.

This then is the original framework on which all Benedictine observance is built. As we see, this framework is notable above all for its simplicity and balance. We can easily understand why, from age to age, monks are always seeking to cast off the complications and additions that have been built on to this simple original structure, and return to the simplicity of the life that was lived by St Benedict himself. At the same time, it is also easy to see that adaptations will always be necessary, and that men will always be changing or modifying the original order of the Benedictine day.

2. *The Benedictines*

The primitive Benedictine observance soon underwent modification. First of all, the monks came in contact with "urban monasticism"— that is with groups of monks, or rather of canons, existing only to furnish choirs for the great Roman basilicas. The sole purpose for the existence of these groups was the praise of God in the divine office. They had none of the monk's labor, obscurity, solitude. Benedictine life, in some monasteries, quickly took on the exclusively liturgical character of these groups, especially when Benedictines themselves were invited to replace canons in the basilicas and cathedrals of the great cities of Christendom. The offices became longer, liturgical ceremonies were added, work was curtailed or ceased to exist, and the monk became intensely conscious of his function as one deputed to carry out with all solemnity the public worship of the Church. Hence arose the conception that the monk existed *propter chorum*, for the choir and nothing else. From being the monk's most important duty, the liturgy finally became his whole life.

Then, within a century of St Benedict's death, the great missionary journeys of the Benedictine monks began. St Augustine was sent to England, soon others would leave England for Germany. The ardor of missionary zeal, the *peregrinationis amor* which drew St Willibrord forth from his cloister at Ripon, became a paradoxical characteristic of saints who had made the Benedictine vow of stability (that is, the vow to live and die in the monastery of their profession).

This was not only a legitimate but a providential adaptation of the Benedictine formula and one which certain clauses of the Rule seemed to anticipate.* The monks had been chosen for the work of spreading the Christian faith and preserving what could be preserved of Roman order and culture. But their vocation was to remain, at it had always been, essentially contemplative, sedentary, and silent.

The combined effect of these two influences —liturgical and missionary—upon the Benedictine life, made itself felt in varying degrees in different monasteries. We must not imagine that all the monks began to spend their whole time

---

* St Benedict allows warmer garments in climates colder than that of Italy, and foresees that his monks may have to live in countries where no vines will grow and wine cannot be obtained. See chapters 55 and 40 of the Rule.

in choir, or their whole time in the pulpit. But from the beginning of the seventh century the monk began to be a member of a large community, devoted to the execution of a more splendid liturgy than Benedict had known, owning large tracts of lands which were cultivated by serfs or hired employees, and devoting himself more to study, writing and teaching than to anything else except liturgical prayer. St Bede is the most charming and most accomplished example of this Benedictine sanctity—Newman has said of him that "in his person and in his writings he is the true type of the Benedictine." St Bede's conception of the monastic life is characteristic of him. What he sought, he said, was "to rest within the enclosure of the monastery and to serve Christ in all security and freedom." He added: "It was ever my delight, besides observing the regular discipline and chanting the office in choir, to be always learning or teaching or writing." * It must not be thought that this was in any sense tainted with what we have come to blame as "activism." Bede was a contemplative, who said: "There is but one theology, which is the contemplation of God, and all other meritorious works and studies of virtue are rightly placed second after this." **

---

* P.L. 90:37.
** *Commentary on St Luke*, chapter 10, P.L. 90.

After St Benedict of Aniane had attempted to codify and firmly establish this type of Benedictine life as the "standard" for all Christian monasticism, and after his attempt had partially failed, Cluny was founded in 910. Cluny was to become the biggest thing that was ever seen in Christendom, but it had obscure and humble beginnings, like any other monastic reform. The ascetic ideal which brought Cluny into existence was stimulated on the one hand by the spectacle of monastic decadence on all sides, and on the other by the fear of the end of the world, which was expected to take place in the year one thousand. Cluny was intended first of all to be a renewal of Benedictine austerity. It emphasized the monk's obligation to separate himself from the world and to live in solitude. It stressed the fact that the monastic life is a life of uninterrupted prayer. To the monks of Cluny, uninterrupted prayer meant almost continual vocal prayer in choir.

The reform soon spread to many of the greatest abbeys in Europe. New foundations were made everywhere. The monastic order was saved. Not only that, but it was now enabled to reach the highest peak of its development. The two thousand Cluniac monasteries became, under St Hugh (1049–1109), the bulwark of Papal power and the main support of St Gregory VII in the sweeping reforms which ushered in the Middle Ages. The political importance of Cluny must not make us forget the sanctity of the life that was led in these monasteries. For two hundred years, the architectural and liturgical splendor of Cluny was only the vesture of an interior sanctity that was beyond question tremendous. Romanesque art, the splendid monastic Churches that still remain in Burgundy, Auvergne and Languedoc, bear witness to the unexampled interior vitality of Cluniac monasticism.

We may be tempted to imagine that the Cluniac ideal was simply the rationalization of a powerful and worldly Christianity, happy to think that riches and splendor were the earthly manifestation of the glories of heaven. But we must look more closely and realize that Cluny was truly and purely Benedictine which is to say that the cornerstone of the whole edifice was, again, humility. Far from being conscious of a glorious career as one probably destined to be a future bishop, the Cluniac realized full well that the monk was one who had chosen the last place in the Church, and had renounced all ecclesiastical honors. Like the Fathers of the Desert, he had left the world with its pomps to fight the obscure battle with the powers of evil which the monk must fight, as Christ fought it, in the desert. Stripped of all hope of hierarchical greatness, the monk's role in the life of the Church is at best invisible. He will never "be" anything or anyone in the sight of men, because his life is hidden with Christ in God.

Great stress was laid, at Cluny, upon monastic silence which is the guarantee of all discipline and regularity. Because Cluny was silent, it was regarded by all as a "paradise" of perfect monastic observance and praised, as such, even by the Carthusians.

Consequently, the monks of Cluny had no hesitation in asserting that their life was truly contemplative. Their contemplation, nourished entirely by the liturgy and the Psalms, was essentially an awareness of God, of Divine Wisdom, living and manifesting himself in the monastic community. The Abbey is not only the Court of Christ, the Great King, but it is the Body of Christ. It is Christ Himself. In other words, the contemplative life of Cluny, liturgical and cenobitic to the very core, was the profound consciousness of the charity of Christ, alive and active in the hearts of all who lived in this enormous community. The "Holy Church of Cluny" was a contemplative monastery because it was a "paradise of charity." Under no other condition could it possibly have been so.

Solesmes

All that was best in the spirit of Cluny still lives in Benedictine monasteries of the Congregations of Beuron, Belgium, Solesmes.

After the Benedictine Order had been practically swept out of existence by the French revolution, it came back to life in 1833 when a French secular priest bought the ruins of St Peter's Abbey, Solesmes, and moved into them with three companions, bringing the seal of the Congregation of St Maur and the antiphonary of the former maurist monastery of Saint Germain des Pres. Dom Prosper Gueranger, a scholar and a liturgist, had a clear and deep intuition into the needs of nineteenth century Christianity and founded the Congregation of Solesmes to carry on a very special work in the Church of God.

The liturgical worship of the Church had declined when the true understanding of the liturgy had become practically extinct. Divorced from its own deepest and most intimate source, Christian piety was sometimes little more than a medley of individualistic devotions. Gregorian chant, if it was sung at all, was so misunderstood that it became a pure caricature of sacred music.

Although he was a contemporary of the Romantics, Dom Gueranger's return to Christian antiquity was something far deeper than artiness

75

or sentiment. He was more than a mere antiquarian. He sensed the need to reawaken the deep consciousness that the life of the Church is the life of Christ; her prayer is the prayer of Christ; her song is the song of Christ. It was a return to the mysticism of Cluny and St Benedict. The monastic "Church" is a mystical Body of men whose function is to lose themselves entirely in the great liturgical mysteries, to forget themselves and their own concerns in order to become entirely absorbed in the *sensus Christi*, the realization of the "charity of Christ which surpasses all knowledge, and to be filled unto all the fullness of God" (Ephesians, 3:19). The monk of Solesmes is before all and above all a "man of the Church" a *vir Ecclesiae*, who contemplates Christ in the mystery of the Church, by which the "manifold wisdom of God is made known to the principalities and powers in heavenly places" (Ephesians, 3:10).

Dom Gueranger expressed this ideal in the following words:

To forget ourselves, and to live in habitual recollection, zealously to plunge our souls into the very beauty of the mysteries, to be interested in every aspect of the supernatural economy according to the inspiration of the Spirit of God who alone can teach us to pray. The words of God, of the saints, as we repeat them over and over again and enter more and more deeply into their meaning, have a supreme grace to deliver the soul sweetly from pre-occupation with itself in order to charm it and introduce it into the very mystery of God and of His Christ. Once we are there, we have only to look and love in all simplicity.

Here again, we are left in no doubt as to the essentially contemplative character of the Benedictine vocation. As his Constitutions tell him, the monk of Solesmes seeks in the monastery "prayer, retirement, the laborious life of the cloister, that he may dwell with God and have in his mind the things of eternity."

What is meant by the laborious life of the cloister? Here Dom Gueranger is not repudiating the traditional conception of monastic quiet and contemplative leisure—but it is a fruitful leisure, in which study and research bring forth results which will be of importance to the whole Church. "The whole monastic life is ordered entirely to contemplation, and the brethren must apply themselves especially to those studies which will nourish and foster in their hearts the spirit of prayer." *

There is some manual labor in the monastery. The monks engage in the usual household tasks, and work sometimes in the gardens or the fields. But their main work is intellectual. A community of the Solesmes congregation is likely to

---

* *Declarationes ad Sanctam Regulam,* c.xx.

be a "team" of research scholars engaged in an important project like, for instance, the new edition of the Vulgate which is slowly being brought out by the monks of St Jerome in the eternal city, the edition of the *Vetus Latina* at Beuron, or the years of research in Gregorian chant done at Solesmes itself since the days of Dom Gueranger.

Solesmes is famous, and there is no need to tell the world the fruitfulness of the work that has been done there. But it must be clearly understood that Solesmes is something more than a monastic university. If there has taken place today a revival of the contemplative life in the Church, we must realize that this is due just as much to the Benedictines of Solesmes and of Marialaach, as to the Trappists and the Carthusians.

Too often those who call themselves contemplatives look with contempt upon the labors of cloistered scholars. But Christian contemplation is nothing at all if it is not nourished by God's revelation of His wisdom in the Mystery of Christ. Christian contemplation is impotent and sterile and illusory if it is not nourished by the sacraments and the theology of the Church. It is the Benedictines of Solesmes, Beuron, and other Congregations, who have brought the other monastic Orders back into direct contact with the great Mystery of Christ as it is revealed in

Scripture and contemplated by the Fathers and the liturgy of the Church.

Nor should we underestimate the discipline, the "asceticism," which goes into this intellectual labor of the monk. Unlike the university scholar, who can envisage a limited "fame" as the author of some weighty dissertation, the monk of Solesmes is likely to be nothing but an obscure and nameless worker in a communal project for which he will never receive any compliments. His individuality is submerged in the work which is done by the community: but if it is submerged, it is not lost. It is sublimated and transfigured spiritually, for here too it is true that every one that humbleth himself shall be exalted and every one that loses his life, for the charity of Christ, shall find it. Here precisely we find the humility that Peter the Venerable felt to be characteristic of Cluny—the humility which is the whole foundation of the spirituality of St Benedict. Self-renunciation for the common good. Self-effacement for the glory of God, and of the "whole Christ."

This involves not the renunciation of responsibility, not an escape from life, but their full acceptance—without any concern for such an inconsequential accident as human applause.

What has been said of the spirit of Solesmes can be applied, with some modification, to the other great Benedictine congregations engaged in study, teaching, and missionary work.

The great American Benedictine Abbeys of the Middle West are massive buildings which bear witness to the German or Swiss ancestry of the various communities. The Archabbey of St Vincent, founded in 1846 at Latrobe, Pennsylvania, is the oldest and most venerable representative of the Benedictine family in the United States. It stands at the head of the American Cassinese congregation, which numbers sixteen abbeys in Minnesota, Kansas, North Carolina, Illinois, Oklahoma, Florida, North Dakota, Washington, Colorado, New Hampshire, Ohio, New Jersey and Saskatchewan.

The Archabbey of St Meinrad in Indiana, founded in 1853 from the Swiss monastery of Einsiedeln, presides over the American Swiss congregation with its nine houses in Missouri, Arkansas, Louisiana, Oregon, Illinois, Wisconsin, South Dakota and British Columbia.

These two congregations came into existence when America was still mission territory, and their spirit is therefore apostolic. The Benedictines have been and are still missionaries among the Indians. They have also erected colleges, schools and seminaries which have trained generations of American priests.

St John's Abbey, founded in 1856 near St Cloud, Minnesota, represents all that is best in the American tradition of the Benedictine Apostolate. Isolated in woodlands between two quiet lakes, St John's is a center of study, prayer, education and the liturgical apostolate. Gardens and farmlands are cultivated by the Brothers and the Clerics, while the priests of the community teach in the High School, University and Diocesan Seminary which are maintained by the Abbey. Two important magazines, *Worship* and *Sponsa Regis* are published at St John's, and the monks also maintain a small publishing house, the Liturgical Press.

The Abbots of St John's have always made it a point never to refuse an appeal to help in the missions. Therefore St John's now maintains dependent monasteries, with schools or missions, in Puerto Rico, the Bahama Islands, Japan, and Mexico. American monks, wearing civilian clothes according to Mexican laws, teach two thousand students in a high school at Tepeyac, a suburb of Mexico City.

One of the most interesting facets of the apostolate at St John's is made evident by the workshops on Pastoral Care and Psychotherapy carried on during the summer. Here Catholic priests from the secular clergy and the religious orders, together with ministers of various Protestant denominations, gather for instructive sessions conducted by outstanding psychiatrists and psychoanalysts from all parts of the country.

So much active zeal and fruitful labor does nothing to alter the fundamentally Benedictine character of the life in our American Abbeys. Here we find the same spirit of worship and work which characterized the Order when St. Gregory sent Benedictine monks to re-Christianize the British Isles. There is perhaps less of the silence and contemplation one might find in monasteries of the Primitive Observance, but the atmosphere remains that of a truly Benedictine community, knit together by the charity of Christ and the spirit of humility and prayer which are essential to the Order.

The states of Minnesota and North Dakota are dotted with parishes founded by the Benedictines, and the country around St. John's resembles parts of Germany or Austria, with nearly every village dominated by the tall spire of a Church built by the monks in pioneer days.

An isolated member of St Ottilien's Missionary Congregation is St Paul's Abbey, Newton, New Jersey. Finally, there exist two independent houses, now foundations of the "Primitive Benedictine Observance," one at Elmira, New York, and the other at Weston, Vermont. We shall say more of these later on.

The English Benedictine Congregation maintains a house of studies, St Anselm's Priory, on the campus of Catholic University at Washington, D.C., and St Gregory's Priory, with its distinguished school at Portsmouth, Rhode Island.

The English Congregation, of which Downside is a good example, adds to this essentially Benedictine spirit a modality of its own which is no less Benedictine and which can be traced back to the seventeenth century Benedictine mystic, Dom Augustine Baker. Here we find a different emphasis, a return to that original, silent, interior prayer which has always been so essential to monastic spirituality. Dom Baker reacted strongly to the irruption of methodical meditations and techniques into the monastic life. Having almost lost his mind, as well as his vocation, from straining his head at these things, he took up arms against the composition of place, methodical considerations and resolutions, and the spiritual nosegay. He preached, instead, that "introversion," or "pure, internal spiritual prayer" was the primary obligation of the monastic life. He recognized clearly that there was an essential difference between monks and canons. The canon is deputed to carry out the divine worship in public, as a public minister of the Church. But the monk chants the divine office as part of his own interior, contemplative life of prayer. The vocation of the canon is to chant the office for the edification of the faithful and the vocation of the monk is to contemplate God. There is a world of difference between the two, and although a canon is by no means automatically excluded from contemplation, a monk who thinks of himself as no more than a canon will fall short of his vocation. As Baker wrote:

It is not for the edification of others (through the liturgy) that a monastical state was instituted. . . . Religious souls truly monastical fly the sight of the world, entering into deserts and solitudes to spend their lives alone in penance and recollection, and to purify their own souls, not to give example and instruction to others. Such solitudes are to be sought by them thereby to dispose themselves for another far more profitable internal solitude, in which creatures being banished, the only conversation is between God and the soul.*

It is true that Baker lacked the full sense of the liturgy and of its relation to contemplative prayer. But there is in reality no contradiction between his emphasis on silent, interior and solitary union with God, and the contemplation which is inspired by the liturgy. In the end, both are the same. One is the fruit of the other. Through the psalms, through the Mass, the monk enters into an inner realization of the Mystery of Christ, and comes to communion with the Father, in the Son, through the power

---

* *Holy Wisdom*, sect. iii, c.4, n.7.

of the Holy Spirit, and this is the contemplation which is the main purpose of the monastic life.

La Pierre Qui Vire

As we turn to the Benedictines of the Primitive Observance—who have congregations in almost every country where the Order flourishes —we find another modality of the monastic life. As its name suggests, the Primitive Observance is stricter, more austere. The liturgical life remains the heart of the observance, but the emphasis is different. Instead of stressing splendor and beauty for God, the monks seek rather to honor Him with the simplicity and poverty of their cult. The Church is plain and austere. Vestments and objects of the cult are simple, even rough. There is more earthenware in the sanctuary than gold or silver, more wool than silk.

There is more stress on manual labor. The monk may still be a scholar, but his scholarship does not usually reach the level of erudition. He studies the riches of Scripture and Tradition, but now no longer as a specialist, as an authority in his chosen field. The monk of the Primitive Observance is more a contemplative than a scholar, even though he may also be a scholar. If he writes, it is rather to share with others the fruits of contemplation than to publish the results of scientific research.

The life is more solitary, more silent. Monasteries of the Primitive Observance are to be looked for off the beaten track, in quiet forests or secluded valleys. The rules of silence are more strict. There are few recreations, or none at all. Fasting and abstinence play a more important part in the life of the monk.

The simple and austere life of the Primitive Observance can rightly claim to come close to the life lived by St Benedict himself, and therefore it has a special attraction of its own. Indeed, it is to the Primitive Observance that vocations are beginning to turn more and more in our day, at least in Europe. In America the Primitive Observance is not yet very well known.

The Abbey of La Pierre qui Vire, the head of the French Congregation of the Primitive Observance, is larger than any other abbey in France today, whether it be Benedictine or Cistercian. The fact that this flourishing and fervent community attracts so many vocations speaks eloquently of the balance and integrity of its observance. The Primitive Benedictines have, indeed, all the advantages of Trappist austerity and of Benedictine discretion. Situated at a mid-point between the observance of Solesmes and the observance of La Trappe, La Pierre qui Vire is a community in which can be found the silence and poverty of the Trappists together with the scholarship, and good taste, and sense of monastic and liturgical values which are the hall-mark of Solesmes. It is a cenobitic life, in which the monk can still enjoy the privacy of his own cell. It is an austere life in which the regime is slightly more benign than that of the Trappists, and therefore it is a life which can be led by one who might not be able to bear the rigors of Trappist life. There is labor and sacrifice, but the work is not so prolonged and arduous as to dull the monk's potentialities for contemplation.

There is at the same time an apostolate of writing and of art, at La Pierre qui Vire: but this apostolate is integrated into the monk's contemplative life, so that it enables him to nourish his spirit by contact with all that is living in the present and in the past. It keeps him conscious of the developments in art, letters and thought, without dragging him into the whirlpool of controversies and intellectual fashions. It is good for the monk to be able to take intelligent note of what is going on in the intellectual and artistic world outside the monastery, and to offer his own discrete and Christian comment, from the vantage point of his solitude.

The question or indeed the problem, of sacred art, is one which has not been ignored by modern monasticism. In some monasteries the study of art has brought forth nothing more than a certain pious dilletantism, a complex of eclectic mannerisms which have done nothing to awaken either a sense of sacredness or a sense of art. At La Pierre qui Vire the monks have been more successful. One feels that there is an undeniable vitality and a true "holiness" in the work of *L'atelier du Coeur Meurtry:* but more than that one is edified by the way in which this work is rooted, so to speak, in the very rocks on which the monastery is built.

Here, first of all, we find a program of communal endeavour, with an essentially medieval outlook in that it focusses all its attention on *things to be made* and on the *intention for which they are made* rather than upon the individual artist and upon his subjective emotions in making them. Here, as in the work that built the monasteries of the eleventh century and the cathedrals of the twelfth and thirteenth, the personality of the craftsman is not publicized. The artist functions as a member of a group which works for the love of God and for the love of the things to be offered to His service, rather than for the fame of the individual artist.

This program demands that the work of art should be the spontaneous fruit of deep and prolonged meditation. It should also spring from patient experimentation in which one has fully come to know the materials he works with. The monastic artist, according to this conception, is a man who is fully aware of what he is doing, why he is doing it, and the things he is doing it with. He even makes his own pigments, from the minerals in his own monastery's land. He paints pictures of the Incarnate Word in colors made from the soil which he tills with his own hands: and the pictures are, as likely as not, for his own monastic church, or perhaps for some parish church or convent in the neighborhood.

The works produced by the studio will, no doubt, be sold. But the artist works rather as a contemplative than as a professional artist. Like all true artists, the monk who paints a fresco or carves a wooden statue thinks above all of the *rightness*, the goodness of the thing he is making, rather than of pleasing the buyer, of fitting in with the theoretical demands of this or that school, or flattering the taste of a public that may not care what is good or bad in art.

Here we see a perfectly valid expression of the Benedictine spirit—a project in which art becomes a means for the salvation of the artist and of those for whom he works. Here, monks make use of the material things God has given them in order to praise God with the work of their hands. Here Benedictine humility is preserved by the sense of one's own limitations and of the limitations of one's material. There is no attempt to make a cheap material look costly.

There is no faking. What is poor will glorify God by the splendor of its poverty.

Zodiaque, a review of sacred art, published by the monks, embraces within its perspectives the Romanesque sculpture of Vezelay or Autun, the primitive art of Africa and Polynesia, and the modern experiments of Braque, Leger, Manessier and Bazaine. Once again, the viewpoint is profoundly contemplative. Avoiding all the mystifications of academic doctrines, whether pious or aesthetic, the eye of the monk goes directly to the spiritual heart of the "sacred" in art. Nor does it hesitate to see through the pretenses or infidelities of routine pietism.

La Pierre qui Vire was founded, curiously enough, by a secular priest with a missionary vocation. When Dom Jean Baptiste Muard died in 1854, four years after the foundation of his monastery, he had travelled a long way both geographically and spiritually.

As a young priest he had dreamed of founding a missionary society which would include hermits and recluses as well as preachers.

At the age of 39, he was thinking of patterning his new society on the Rule of St Francis. He started out on foot for Italy to study the religious life. He found his way to the monastery of Subiaco, and there he was permitted to live as a hermit in the ruins of one of St Benedict's original twelve foundations, a little chapel perched half way up the side of a cliff. Here he decided that the Rule for his foundation would be the Rule of St Benedict. Father Muard returned to France, and made his novitiate at the Trappist monastery of Aiguebelle. Then he purchased a tract of forest land in a wild corner of Burgundy called the Morvan. The monastery was built, in the middle of a forest, on a granite hillside. Dom Muard still had the notion of making it a center of missionary activity, and indeed the monks became known to the peasants as "Trappist preachers." However, Dom Muard at last abandoned this plan, and La Pierre qui Vire has since remained a monastery of contemplatives whose apostolic radiation is silent, and reaches out from within the monastery more powerfully by its prayers than by the printed word.

Until recently, North America had known only the Benedictines of the great missionary congregations we have mentioned above—institutes that have played such a considerable part in the Christianization of the United States. There is also in Canada a monastery of the Solemes Congregation—Saint Benoit du Lac—which has carried on quietly the distinguished tradition of liturgy, scholarship and chant which we have learned to associate with the name of Solesmes. Beautifully situated in forest lands of the Province of Quebec, Saint Benoit du Lac was for a long time the only representative of the cloistered and contemplative Benedictine life in North America.

The first appearance of "Primitive Benedictinism" on this continent was in Mexico when Dom Gregorio Lemercier founded his Monastery of the Resurrection at Cuernavaca, Morelos. This small community made up entirely of Mexican Indians (except for the Superior) is one of the most remarkable and courageous experiments in modern monastic history. Struggling against desperate odds, living under very primitive conditions in true poverty and simplicity, depending on the labor of their hands and the Providence of God, the monks of Cuernavaca are perhaps closer to St Benedict than anyone else on this side of the Atlantic.

Since 1950, the Primitive Observance has also appeared in the United States. Dom Damasus Winzen, founder of Mount Saviour, on a wooded hill outside Elmira, New York, made his profession at Marialaach, in the Rhineland. Formed by Dom Ildefons Herwegen, and nourished by the purest sources of monastic tradition, a student of Scripture and the Fathers, Dom Damasus has attempted to return to the primitive simplicity of St Benedict. In doing so he has broken to some extent with the ideal of Marialaach which is primarily a "kulturabtei"— a home of scholarship and liturgy. Mount Saviour is something else. Dom Damasus is trying to return to the very early monasticism in which the monk was purely and simply a monk, and not also a priest or cleric. According to his plan, there are to be only a few priests in the monastery, and no laybrothers. The bulk of the community will be made up of monks: that is to say of religious who have been tonsured, and have assumed the obligation of chanting the office in choir, but who spend their days in manual labor rather than in study, the preaching of retreats, the hearing of confessions, and other activities more proper to priests. Obviously, the Benedictine balance between choral prayer, manual labor, and meditative reading will be preserved above all: but the majority of the "choir religious" will never have a thought of any liturgical or pastoral care that belongs to the priesthood.

It is of course a very great thing that large monastic communities like the Trappist monastery of Gethsemani, for instance, should have many priests in the choir. But there remains a very great need for the particular kind of monastic life which has been planned at Mount Saviour. That life cannot actually be found anywhere else. Many who apply for admission to Trappist monasteries as laybrothers are, in fact, looking for the pure monastic life—the life of the monk who is not a cleric. Yet the life of a laybrother falls somewhat short of this. At the same time, it is a matter of experience that some young choir monks, in the conventional monastic set-up, lose their vocations when they leave the novitiate and enter upon their clerical studies.

It is clear that the experiment at Mount Saviour is aimed at filling a serious gap in the monastic life today.

The other Primitive Benedictine monastery in the United States is at Weston, Vermont. It is a dependency of the monastery of the Dormition in Jerusalem, and its members also lead a life of monastic simplicity, labor and prayer, without any apostolic ministry. A peculiar feature of this community is that its members may be called upon, at any time, to go to the Mother Abbey in the Holy Land. The monastery of the Dormition is the shrine at the place where Our Lady is believed to have "fallen asleep" in the Lord and rested in death before her Assumption.

3. *The Cistercians*

It is customary to begin discussions of Cistercian spirituality with a historical flourish, and to state that on Palm Sunday 1098 Robert of Molesmes and his companions left their Benedictine monastery and retired to the woods of Citeaux in order to follow the Rule of St Benedict "to the letter." The expression "to the letter" is the starting point of heated discussions, in which the Cistercians are accused of pharisaism, literalism, fanaticism, or praised for their austere integrity. The result of such discussions has always been to obscure some of the main features of the Cistercian character. The Cistercians certainly wanted to return to the austere simplicity of Benedictine life, for they believed that St Benedict had effectively codified the renunciation and charity of the early Christians. They saw in the Rule of St Benedict the *formula perfectae penitentiae* * (the formula of perfect penance, or perfect conversion) which

---

* *Exordium Magnum*, Dist. 1, cap. 1. Cf. *Waters of Siloe*, p. 19.

would enable the monk to live the Gospel and become transformed in Christ.

A casual glance at any of the writings of the Cistercian Fathers, or at the earliest legal documents of the Order, will show that Cistercian austerity was not considered an end in itself but a means of putting off the "old man" corrupted by sin, and renewing the image of God, implanted by the Creator in the soul of His creature, by perfect likeness to Christ in Charity.

The Cistercian reform aimed, then, to restore the pure charity of the early Christians by means of a simple and austere common life, in which the monks, "poor with the poor Christ—*pauperes cum paupere Christo*—" living in community, sharing their poverty and labor and prayer and praise, would come to union with God by loving one another as Christ had loved them. This life was therefore and above all deeply contemplative—a life "in the Spirit"—and the monastic community was a City of God in the building, its members were living stones, built together by charity into an "habitation of God in the Spirit" (*Ephesians*, 2:22).* The

---

* This theme is developed most clearly in St Bernard's sermons for the Dedication of the Church of Clairvaux (Migne P.L. 183, 517). The visible Church made of stones is but the sacrament (symbol) of the invisible and real Church which is the monastic community itself, made up of souls in the image of God, in whom the ceremonies performed by the bishop at the dedication are mystically performed by Christ, through the action of the Holy Spirit. Their responsibility is to co-

Cistercian life is essentially a life of contemplation in common, in which the humility, poverty and charity of the common life are regarded above all as means to dispose the soul remotely for union with God in mystical wisdom.

Once these essential overtones of charity and contemplation are forgotten the *Exordium Parvum* and the other fundamental statements of Cistercian policy refuse to yield us their true meaning. In fact, it is quite easy to squabble about the degree of austerity that was originally intended by the Cistercian Fathers, to lose oneself in hairsplitting details about clothing, food and sources of income, and finally to overlook completely the "one thing that is necessary" to make a true Cistercian, which is contemplative charity.

Charity is, of course, no monopoly in any religious Order. It is the soul of all religious perfection. In determining the nature of the Cistercian spirit, we must decide what is the peculiar modality of charity for a Cistercian. We have seen that the charity of a life of labor and poverty, lived in common, is meant to prepare the monk for contemplative union with God.

---

operate with this action, working to produce unity within themselves, unity with their brethren by charity, and union with God, Who seeks to dwell perfectly in the temple of each individual soul and in the great temple which is made up of all their souls in One.

What are some of the other aspects of the Cistercian life?

The monks live in community, it is true: but there is a constantly recurring emphasis on solitude. The community is hidden in the wilderness, far from the world. In the *Exordium Parvum* Citeaux is spoken of as an hermitage (*eremus*), contrasted with the cenobium of Molesme. This does not mean that the first Fathers of Citeaux considered themselves hermits. With the possible exception of St Robert of Molesme (who had several times withdrawn from a cenobium to become a hermit) the Cistercian Fathers were all adamant in their devotion to the common life. But that the community itself should withdraw and live in solitude was an essential function of Cistercian poverty and humility. Here is how Isaac de l'Etoile spoke to his monks, in one of the more remote monasteries of the Order, founded on an island in the Atlantic:

For this reason, my dearly beloved, we have led you all away into this remote and arid and vile solitude; and we have done it wisely, in order that here you may be humble, and *never be able to become rich*. Yes, here in this solitude, cast far out into the sea and having almost nothing in common with the rest of the world, destitute of all human and worldly consolation, you have become totally silent from the world. For indeed, here, look where you will, you see that you have no world left at all except this poor little island, the last extremity of the earth.*

The monk who lives in solitude is far out of reach of the rich benefactors who have spoiled other monasteries with their well-meaning generosity. He is forced to work, and work hard, to support himself. Also, he is obliged to share the fruits of his labor with the other poor men around him. He has loved poverty and solitude not for their own sakes, but for the sake of Christ. He sees Christ mystically present in the poor, and has sought union with Christ by identification with Him in the poor. Sharing the labors of the poor, dividing the fruits of one's work with them establishes the monk in a kind of mystical unity with the "poor Christ." This concept is the key to the whole Cistercian theology of labor, and it is for this that the Cistercian works with his hands—not for exercise, or for the love of agriculture, or for mere ascetic self-improvement. Isaac continues, addressing the Lord:

O Lord, here solitude has been piled upon solitude and silence has been added to silence. For in order that we may be more able and accustomed to speak with Thee, we are silent with one an-

---

* Isaac de l'Etoile, *Sermon xiv*, (2nd Sermon for the IVth Sunday after Epiphany), Migne, P.L. 194-1757.

other. But, my brethren we must thank God and praise Him for His mercy, for we have hoped in Him and His mercy has descended upon us. He has deigned to give us this exile as a place that is just right for us, so that we are free to read and pray and meditate, and yet are forced to work. Thus we do not lack a chance to give something to the poor.*

St Bernard permits the Cistercian to seek physical solitude at times and to go apart from the rest of his brethren for the sake of silent and solitary prayer: "O holy soul, remain alone! Keep thyself for Him alone thou hast chosen for thyself among all others. . . . It is profitable for thee to separate thyself even bodily, when thou canst, especially in the time of private prayer." ** In giving this counsel, the abbot of Clairvaux cites the example of Christ Himself withdrawing from His disciples to pray alone on the mountain. But in general Cistercian solitude is not valued purely for the opportunities of silent and peaceful prayer that it offers. It is a function of poverty, and it is more or less relative. The interior freedom and recollection which the Cistercian seeks are procured not merely by withdrawal but by patience and obe-

---

* Ibid.
** *Et corpore interdum non otiose te separes cum opportune potes, prassertim tempore orationis.* Serm. 40 *In Cantica,* n.4. Cf. our discussion of this point, *Waters of Siloe,* p. 343 ff.

dience and mortification and labor—all of which are the lot of the poor man.

We cannot quite understand the Cistercian Fathers if we overlook the fact that they were juridically minded, that their sense of Law endowed them with an extraordinary practicality. Nowhere, even in St Benedict himself, do we find such a well developed juridical structure as we do in the foundation of the Cistercian Order. Indeed, this is why it is not only the first religious Order in the strict sense of the word, but was also chosen, by the Jurist Pope Innocent III to serve as a model to all other Orders, in its organizational framework.

The Jurist of the Order was an Englishman, St Stephen Harding, author of the *Exordium Parvum* and framer of the Charter of Charity. I call him a jurist to emphasize the fact that he had an extremely well developed sense of *Jus*, of Law and of Right, rather than a mere knowledge of legal prescriptions. Indeed, Stephen Harding not only possessed an instinctive, prudential alertness to the demands of God's will as expressed in the Sacred Canons, but was also a rare and indeed admirable being—a mystic of the Law. That is to say that he had arrived at the almost miraculous synthesis of Law and Charity, the ability to see the prescriptions of the sacred canons intact and whole in the Love by which they are dictated and in which they are fullfilled. As another Cistercian, Adam of Perseigne, has said, "Law is love which binds and obliges" (*Lex est amor qui ligat et obligat*). Stephen himself pointed out in the *Exordium Parvum* that the Fathers and Popes who had laid down the norms by which monks should live by their own labor had spoken as "organs of the Holy Spirit." *

In seeking to restore the primitive Benedictine life, St Stephen Harding was therefore not merely striving to pacify his conscience by bringing his life into perfect conformity with the written code by which he had vowed to live. He was going much deeper into the reality of things: and here we might as well remark that nowhere in the *Exordium Parvum* does St Stephen use the phrase the "letter of the Rule." On the contrary, what he speaks of is *rectitudo regulae* and the *puritas regulae*, the "integrity of the rule, the "purity of the rule." These words embrace not only the letter but also the spirit, and indicate that St Stephen realized the rule was not merely an external standard to which one's actions had to conform, but a *life* which, if it was lived would transform the monk from within. And so, as a matter of fact, instead of violently forcing the monks of Citeaux into a servile acceptance of the letter of the Rule, pre-

---

* *Exordium Parvum*, c.15.

cisely as it was written, nothing more and nothing less, St Stephen actually brought about an adaptation of the Rule to twelfth century conditions which was the work of religious genius. There are in fact many things in the Cistercian observance which are not found in the "letter" of the rule but which belong to its "rectitudo" and "puritas." One of them is the institution of lay-brethren, another is the exclusion of child-oblates from the monastery, so that the monks would not be saddled with the responsibility of educating young children. The Cistercian day varied slightly from the horarium of St Benedict, the principal addition being that of a daily Conventual Mass, and sometimes of two such masses. Stephen also prescribed the institution of the Office of the Dead which had come over from Cluny. But he cast aside all the other "little offices," litanies, processions, and other accretions which made the Cluniac office so long and—as even Peter the Venerable admitted—so tedious.

The Cistercians preferred to cut down the office to its original simplicity, in order to have plenty of time for work in the fields. Once again, the liturgy was reduced to the proportions that befitted the life of poor men and cultivators of the soil.

In all things we find the early Cistercians preoccupied with the *reality* of the monastic life.

They were indefatigable in their search for the genuine, for the authentic. Stephen Harding spared no trouble and expense to have two brethren travel to Metz and to Milan to bring back the pure texts of the Gregorian chant which they would sing in the office. He himself set about a revision of the Vulgate in order that the text of the Lessons might be more correct.

St Bernard came to build on this solid foundation the loftiest mystical structure that has ever risen within the Benedictine enclosure. He too would speak of "Law." He too would be a mystic of "Law." But going beyond Stephen Harding he would gaze into the depths of God Himself and discover that God too has a "Law," which is His own infinite charity, His own freedom, His own generosity. He would see that this Law of God entered into the world not only by creating all things and implanting itself in their natures, but above all in the Incarnation of the Word Who was to redeem fallen man by the supreme expression of His infinite liberty, in which He, Who was without sin, took upon Himself the sins of men out of pure and gratuitous love, and for their sakes became "obedient unto the death of the Cross." (Phil. 2:8)

The Law of divine Liberty, hidden and active in the Person of Christ, broke into the world of sin in which man languished as a prisoner of a far different Law, the Law of cupidity and self-ishness. Christ showed man the way to escape from the bondage of his own self-hood, and gave him the power to make that escape by the grace which flows from the Cross into the free wills of men, strengthening their liberty so that they can not only avoid evil and choose the spiritual and eternal good, but can become like unto God Himself by the perfection of a sacrifice of pure love which reproduces in their lives the Sacrifice of the Cross.

The Cistercian monastery is, therefore, in the eyes of St Bernard, a school of Christ. That is as much as to say that it is a school of pure love and of perfect liberty. It is a place in which the soul rediscovers its own inborn nobility and integrity as a child of God, and learns to exercise that freedom and love for which it was created in the image and likeness of Him Who is Charity Itself.

The *Ordo* (Order, or observance,) of the Cistercian life, is there as the necessary pedagogue and guardian of the soul of the monk. It shows him the limits within which he must confine his exterior and bodily activity, in order that he may not stray away from the sphere of influence of the Holy Spirit. The *Ordo* of the Cistercian is therefore abjection and humility, voluntary poverty and obedience but also peace

and joy in the Holy Spirit, says St Bernard.*
He continues:

Our *Ordo*, our observance, is to be under a
Master, under an Abbot; under a rule, under discipline. Our Ordo is the practice of silence, exercise in fasting, vigils, prayers; manual labor. *But
above all it is to hold to the more excellent way,*
which is charity, and indeed to progress in all these
things from day to day, and to persevere in them
until the last day.**

Fidelity to the austere Cistercian observance
is the condition which enables the monk to open
his soul to the silent, inward teaching of Christ.
By keeping the Rule and obeying his Abbot, he
places himself at the feet of Christ, the only true
teacher of the interior life, and he takes his seat,
as it were, in the classroom of the Holy Spirit—
auditorium Spiritus. Mere physical presence in
the monastery is not enough to make a man the
disciple of Christ. Mere listening to the instruc-
tions of an abbot, be he St Bernard himself, will
not make him a saint. Nor does the external fulfillment of the prescriptions of the Rule accomplish the real work of monastic perfection. That
work must be done in the soul of the monk by
the Holy Spirit, who speaks only to the humble.
Therefore, says St Bernard, "He who places his

---

* *Epistola* 142, # 1—Migne P.L. 182:297.
** Ibid.

trust in any other religious practice, any other meritorious action, any other wisdom than in humility alone, is not only a fool but insane." *

St Bernard is very practical in his idea of humility. It is not the self-complacency of a soul that feels itself to be perfect in the sight of God and obscure in the eyes of men. This is a travesty of true humility which does not exist without compunction, that is to say without a burning sense of our own imperfection. Yet at the same time true humility is calm and peaceful. It accepts our limitations, it is not surprised at imperfection or even at sin. The proud man is astonished when he commits a fault, and because he is proud he cannot forgive himself any blemish. For the proud forgive themselves nothing. They conceal from their own sight whatever they cannot bear in themselves, and if they cannot conceal it they die of shame. But the humble man, as St Bernard says, profits by his weaknesses and sins. If he breaks the rule, he realizes that:

It is a good thing to fall if by the rebuke of a just man the one who falls rises to his feet and his sin falls to the ground. For then the Lord rises upon the sin, trampling it under foot and stamping it down lest it rise again.**

---

* Sermon 26, P.L. 182:610.
** Sermon 54, In Cantica, n.6 P.L. 182:1052.

In St Bernard's mind, the Rule of St Benedict must be observed with generosity and discretion at the same time. The true monk cannot gloss over prescriptions and observances as if they were trivial. If he neglects them, he runs the risk of losing his true sense of spiritual values and becoming a worldly and materialistic person, a monk in name only. On the other hand, not all the points of the Rule are equally important. The monk must learn how to distinguish between them by "the secret instinct of a devout and sincere soul." * This "instinct" which is a practical intuition that is already related to "wisdom," teaches the monk to observe carefully those prescriptions which are most important, without despising those which are of less importance.

Discretion will teach the monk the difference between the precepts and the remedies which are contained in the Rule. But he cannot see the difference between them if everything appears to him to be a precept, and if he imagines that it is possible for him to keep the whole Rule all the time without sometimes failing through weakness or inadvertence. This point is important, because when it is not understood it leads the monk either into illusion or into despair. The Rule of St Benedict is not supposed to be

---

* "*Intimo quodam devoti sincerique animi sapore . . .*" *De Praecepto et Dispensatione*, c.7, n.16. Migne. P.L. 182:869.

observed in the way the Pharisees observed the mosaic Law. On the contrary, it is meant to remind us of our human frailty and keep us humble. We are sanctified not merely by the precepts we keep, but by those which we inadvertently break, provided that we make use of the remedies which the Rule provides.

The keen ascetic eye of St Bernard, who was not only a psychologist but a saint, endowed with the charismatic gift of the discernment of spirits, saw how prone some souls would be to pervert the austerities of the Rule and make them the instruments of pharasaical vanity. This is the professional risk which must be assumed by everyone who embraces the monastic life. The temptation does not present itself in the form of obvious and conscious hypocrisy. It is manifest, rather, in an unconscious anxiety, a spirit of fear and suppressed jealousy, which leads monks to seek security and strength in their own practices, prayers and experiences. In order to feel secure in their own observance, they tend to belittle the observance of others.

This is the problem which St Bernard tackles at the beginning of his *Apologia*, in which he laments the monastic rivalry between Citeaux and Cluny. If there are Cistercians who have tried to belittle the observance of Cluny as "soft" and relaxed, they are greatly to be pitied, says St Bernard. For if they say such things, it means that they have not the spirit of monks. And in that case, their fasts, vigils, labor, poverty are without value. If we secretly glory in these things, as if by themselves they made us great and holy men, then we are implicitly doing them "in order to be seen by men." We are seeking temporal glory. We deserve the reproach of St Paul, who said "If in this life only we hope in Christ we are the most miserable of all men" (I Corinthians, 15:19).

St Bernard adds a characteristic comment: "Could we not have found for ourselves a more pleasant road to hell? If it is necessary for us to go there why don't we at least choose the broad path, which is followed by so many, and which leads to death, so that we might pass from joy to grief, instead of grieving all the way to hell." And he adds: "Woe to those who carry the Cross of Christ and do not follow Christ: to those who share in His sufferings, and yet refuse to follow Him in His humility." *

The rule therefore does not exist merely to enable us to perform difficult actions and acquire unusual virtues, but also and above all to show us how to make use of our faults. The austere observances of the monastic life are not designed to make us look great in our own eyes and in the eyes of others, but to show us our

---

* Apologia, c.1, n.2 P.L. 182, 899.

own infirmities, and teach us to compassionate the weaknesses and limitations of other men. The true purpose of the Rule is not to blind us to reality and sever our contact with our brothers, but to open our eyes to the universal weakness and helplessness of man, and show us our need of one another and of God's mercy. Benedictine humility will therefore teach the monk not to conceal his frailties under a rigid and punctilious exterior conduct, but to use them as means for arriving at union with God by humility and compassion, and above all by an ever growing faith in the divine mercy. It is for this reason that St Benedict after enumerating all the "instruments of good works" which the monk will use in the ascetic workshop of the monastery, gives the last and in some sense most important place to trust in the mercy of God—*de Dei misericordia numquam desperare.**

In the language of medieval asceticism, the clear-sighted recognition and mature acceptance of our own limitations is called "compunction." Compunction is a spiritual grace, an insight into our own depths which, in one glance, sees through our illusions about ourselves, sweeps aside our self-deceptions and daydreams, and shows us ourselves exactly as we are. But at the same time it is a movement of love and free-

---

* Rule, chapter 4.

dom, a liberation from falsity, a glad and grateful acceptance of the truth, with the resolution to live in contact with the deep spiritual reality which has been opened up to our vision: the reality of God's will in our own lives.

The monk, then, desires to acknowledge his limitations, and he seeks to recognize his faults with a burning compunction that purifies him of sin. Compunction can indeed be a mystical grace, a fire "which is God Himself, which consumes but does not afflict. It burns sweetly, it produces a delightful desolation. It acts at the same time as fire upon our vices and as ointment upon our souls." St Bernard concludes that this mystical perfection of humility is the sign of Christ's presence and action purifying the heart of the monk from within, "When you experience this power which totally changes you, and the love which sets you on fire, understand that the Lord is present in your heart." *

The fruit of humility and compunction is interior peace, which is nothing but the realization of our true selves, as we actually are, in Christ. It establishes us in solid faith, and roots our whole being not in the shifting sand of our own talents and qualities but in the deep firm soil of Christ's mercy. Then, as St Bernard says "When the soul has found the truth in itself, or

---

* Sermon 57, in Cantica, n.7. P.L. 183, 1053.

rather has found itself in the truth it can say
'I believed, therefore have I spoken . . .' " *

This is the perfection of what St Bernard calls
"discipline"—it is the beginning of the interior
life. Without discipline and humility, the monk
cannot grow and become spiritually mature. He
cannot go on to the next stage, in which he
learns to live at peace with others, until he has
first learned to live at peace with himself. Still
less can he ascend to the supreme, undisturbed
tranquility of mystical prayer.

Here we must remark that although it is the-
oretically possible for every monk to arrive at
mystical union with God, St Bernard knows
well that in practice many will remain fixed at
lower degrees of the spiritual life. Each must remain where he is capable of finding peace. Some
find peace only in active works of penance.
Others find their peace in obedience and in the
obscurity of the common life. Still others are at
peace when they can serve others in works of
mercy. The difference between these states depends not only on the choice and efforts of the
individual, but on a special call of God.**

Some will receive graces of contemplation

---

* De Gradibus Humilitatis, n.15, P.L. 182, 949.
** "*Non omnibus in uno loco frui datur grata et secreta
Sponsi praesentia, sed ut cuique paratum est a Patre ipsius.
Non enim nos eum elegimus, sed ipse elegit nos, et posuit nos,
et ubi quisque positus est, ibi est.*" Sermon 23, in Cantica, n.9
P.L. 183:889.

for themselves alone, others will be filled with wisdom for themselves and for others. These will then receive some charismatic function in the community, leading and guiding their brethren in the ways of divine union. But few are called to such a state, because few will have the necessary combination of discretion and contemplative wisdom.

There are few [he says] who are useful as superiors, and fewer still who are humble superiors. In order to be both useful and humble, one must have perfectly obtained that mother of virtues, discretion, and at the same time be inebriated with the wine of charity to the point of contemning one's own glory, of completely forgetting oneself, and of never seeking one's own interests (in preference to those of others). This is something which can only be had by the special and extraordinary action of the Holy Spirit within the wine-cellar of contemplation. For the virtue of discretion, without the fervor of charity, is limp and useless, while vehement, indiscrete fervor leads to ruin.*

Cistercian mysticism is fully realistic. It is not a quest for exalted subjective experiences, but a search for Christ. It seeks Him in faith, it finds Him in His mercy, it knows Him in perfect charity. The Cistercian life is the attempt to plumb all the depths of the theology of the

---

* Sermon 23, in Cantica, n.9. P.L. n.8 col. 888.

Gospel and Epistle of St John, who said
"Everyone that loveth is born of God, and
knoweth God. He that loveth not, knoweth not
God, for God is charity" (I John 4:7-8). And
Jesus said: "This is my commandment that you
love one another as I have loved you . . . He
that hath my commandments and keepeth them;
he it is that loveth me. And he that loveth me,
shall be loved of my Father, and I will love
him, and will manifest myself to him" (John
15:12, 14:21). Whether or not he may be called
to the secret ecstasy of mystical union, every
Cistercian monk is invited to the "wedding
feast" of perfect charity.

St Bernard finds all this symbolized and prefigured in the Marriage Feast of Cana, which
typifies the Christian life, and especially the life
of monks. We fill the waterpots with water, for
"purification," when we are faithful to the austere observances of the Order—silence, fasting,
vigils, psalmody, manual labor and ascetic purity of heart.* Then Christ Himself comes, and
by the action of His Holy Spirit transforms the
water of our observance into the wine of charity. We share the wine of charity with one another, our hearts burning with compassion and
transported with spiritual joy, as we begin to
discover Christ in one another. But the Marriage

---

* Sermon 55 De Diversis.

itself is the Marriage of Christ and the Church. Each one of us, individually, is called to the "mystical Marriage" which unites us to Christ individually and as a group, as the "Church"; for, says St Bernard, "We indeed are the Spouse —all together we form one Spouse, and the souls of each one of us are as it were single spouses." * The perfection of the marriage consists in loving Him as He has loved us. *Qui perfecte diligit, nupsit.***

The fact that Christ ardently desires this marriage with His Church, that He has descended from heaven and died on the Cross in order to win her for His mystical Bride, is the whole reason for the call to the Cistercian cloister. The Cistercian life is a constant purification of love, in the individual and in the community, so that Christ may find on earth the selfless charity which reflects the joy and purity of heaven.

Cistercian devotion to the Incarnate Word and to the Blessed Virgin Mary are to be seen in this context. Jesus is the Word made Flesh, Who has made Himself accessible to our minds and hearts of flesh, since without the Incarnation and the Cross we never could have grasped the charity of God for men. But the love for

---

* Sermon 2 for the 1st Sunday after Epiphany, n.2 P.L. 183:158.

** "He who loves perfectly, has become married." Serm. 83 in cantica. n3, P.L. 183:1182.

Christ as Man is only the beginning of an ascent which discovers in Him the Word, consubstantial with the Father, and the Head of His Mystical Body, the Church. Mary is the fountain of compassion and grace who stands silent and invisible in the midst of the Cistercian community, as she once did at the Marriage of Cana, begging the Lord to have mercy on us when the wine of the spirit, the wine of compassion and charity and faith, comes to fail.

It has been necessary to develop, at some length, these theological notions for without them the Cistercian life will never really make sense. If we do not remember that the Cistercian comes to the monastery above all to seek Christ, and to imitate and reproduce in his life the perfect charity of Christ, his fasts, labors, poverty and solitude become nothing but ascetic feats which we can admire or not, according to our dispositions. Above all, if the monk himself does not know the reason for his vocation, he cannot find the peace of the monastic life which is promised him when he enters the monastery. For the peace of the monastic life does not rest on ascetic or mystical achievements, but on faith in the mercy of God, selfless compassion for our brethren, and pure love for the Father, in union with the charity of Christ.

It is obvious that these things are not peculiar to Cistercians. They are proper to the monastic vocation as such, and common to all Christians. But the whole reason for the Cistercian common life is to purify the monk of selfishness in the most complete and effective way. It is therefore clear that the asceticism of the common life is a delicately balanced instrument which does not produce its results unless it is handled with a certain amount of respect. This respect cannot exist in a hard heart. The common life does not sanctify men who have let themselves become machines. They must remain men, and they must retain a certain affection towards one another if they are to practice true charity. They must be interested in one another, and at the same time they must respect the inmost needs of their brothers' souls. They must learn how to show compassion for one another without being obtrusive, to help one another without being nuisances, and to sustain the weak without being officious or patronizing. The true Cistercian is one who not only knows when to keep silent, and how to keep silent, but when to speak and how to speak, when to show sympathy and how to show it.

So much for the interior aspects of the Cistercian life. Now, what about its exterior and material framework? What do the monks do? How do they live?

The Cistercians simply try to keep as close as possible to the original plan of St. Benedict.

They rise in the small hours of the morning (2:00 or 2:15) and begin at once to chant the Canonical Office of Vigils. This is followed by a half-hour of meditation and the Office of Lauds. Then comes a long stretch of an hour and a half or two hours, about dawn, when the priests of the monastery say their Masses in private, when the Brothers and Students receive communion, and when all apply themselves to *Lectio Divina* (meditative reading.) A light breakfast of bread and coffee is taken before Prime, which is chanted at 6:15. This is followed by the daily Chapter, where the monks gather for a spiritual discourse by the Father Abbot and accuse themselves of their faults against the Rule.

After Chapter there is another period of *Lectio Divina* followed by Tierce and the Conventual Mass, which is always sung in full, every day. There are then some two hours of manual labor in the morning, and two or two and one-half hours in the afternoon. The monks work in the fields or shops, intellectual work being unusual in a Trappist monastery. Dinner is taken after the office of Sext, at 11:30, and everyone knows how restricted the Trappist diet is. No meat, fish, or eggs are served in the general portions of the community. Only the sick receive such things. The rest rely on milk, cheese, and vegetables. If Trappists do not eat meat or fish, they at least have a reputation for baking very good bread and making excellent cheese. Many of the monasteries in America have taken to selling their bread and cheese to the general public, and largely support themselves in this manner.

The Trappist work-day ends in the evening when the monk again returns to his reading, then chants Vespers and Compline before retiring at 7 o'clock along with the birds.

The above plan of the Cistercian day differs slightly from what used to be familiar. The General Chapter of 1954 reduced the number of vocal prayers recited in common. The Little Office of the Blessed Virgin, which used to be chanted in choir every day along with the Canonical office, has been commuted to an antiphon and collect sung before each canonical hour. Otherwise the horarium is roughly the same as it always was, there being a little more time now provided for *Lectio Divina*.

The traditional austerities of the Trappists have also been somewhat moderated in recent years, but there is no question of mitigation. Milk and cheese are now allowed even in Lent (when before they were forbidden), and fifteen minutes have been added to the monk's sleep. The Trappist day remains, on the whole, an arduous one with plenty of hard work and long hours in choir. The monastic setting is one of great simplicity and poverty, in which little thought is given to bodily comfort. The monks are bound by a strict rule of silence. They never converse with one another, and speak only to their Superiors and then only when necessary. They rarely leave the monastery, and sometimes spend years or indeed a whole lifetime without ever seeing the nearest small town. Newspapers and radios are unknown inside the monastery, and only sparse fragments of the world's news reach the ears of the monks.

The Cistercian monk is able, in a word, to get along without many things which others deem to be real necessities. His happiness is not diminished in any way. On the contrary, these silent monasteries are now well known as the home of truly happy men. The life is difficult, no doubt, but the faith and self-sacrifice which make it possible also fill the heart of the monk with a peace which the world cannot give.

The real hardship of the Cistercian life is psychological and interior, and for that reason no one with weak nerves or neurotic tendencies should be encouraged to enter a Trappist monastery. To live successfully in the silence of the Cistercian cloister, one must have enough maturity to face the real problems of the interior life instead of evading them and camouflaging them. Such problems are to be solved in the darkness of faith, in the silence of true humility, and in the poverty of a spirit that is willing to be emptied of its self-complacency and to be content when it sees nothing in itself that it can admire.

It is well known that the strict Cistercian life has attracted many vocations in modern America, and it can be said without exaggeration that not all those who have entered Cistercian monasteries have quite known what they were looking for, and many have not found exactly what they were looking for. Those who thought they wanted sacrifice have perhaps found sacrifices that they did not expect. Those who wanted to live in the simplicity and charity of the Gospel have found the opportunity to do what they sought.

The Cistercian family today is divided into two large groups. The Cistercians of the Strict Observance, or Trappists, are a homogeneous, unified religious Order. The Cistercians of the Common Observance are a loose-knit group of Congregations following different observances.

One of the most interesting monasteries attached to the Common Observance today is the ancient Abbey of Boquen, in Brittany, revived in 1936 by Dom Alexis Presse. A scholar and lover of austerity, with the tenacious and energetic soul of a Breton, Dom Alexis started by living as a hermit in the ruins of this old abbey, lost in the wilderness miles from any road. When the postman of the nearest village found

a letter in his bag addressed to the Abbey of Boquen he thought he was the victim of a joke.
But Dom Alexis soon made his presence known.
He was joined by companions, and they began
rebuilding the ruined monastery.

Boquen is now the center of the strictest and
most austere Cistercian observance, one which
has swept aside all the adaptations, whether
strict or light, which have been made in the Cistercian Usages since the twelfth century. From
Boquen on down, the Common Observance
then runs the gamut of all imaginable interpretations of the Cistercian way of life. One of the
most satisfactory is no doubt the observance followed at the Swiss monastery of Hauterive
where, in the original spirit of Cîteaux, and with
the genuine balance of the Cistercian horarium,
the contemplative life is lived without excessive
austerity, but in solitude and peace.

The great monasteries of the Common Observance are still to be found in Bavaria, Austria, and Switzerland. Hungary too, before the
coming of Communism, was one of the strong-
holds of the Cistercian Common Observance.
The chief monastery of the "Sacred Cistercian
Order" in America is a foundation of the Hun-
garian Abbey of Zirc: it is the Priory of Spring
Bank, in Wisconsin.

The rapid rise of the Cistercians of the Strict
Observance in the United States in the last

twenty years has been a rare and important phenomenon in monastic history. The time has not yet come to evaluate the importance of the movement. Quantitatively, it has now passed its peak. But monastic history is not made by numbers and statistics and everything depends on the spiritual quality of the residue. There have been literally hundreds of vocations in the big American Abbeys of Gethsemani and Spencer and in their more important foundations. Of these hundreds, as was to be expected, more than half did not remain in the monastery. The generation of those who remained are now reaching their religious maturity and are ready to play an active part in the monastic destinies of America.

Foundations continue to be made. The Abbey of Our Lady of the Valley, in Rhode Island, burned down in 1950 and moved to a spacious and handsome new monastery at Spencer, Massachusetts. Our Lady of Guadalupe, founded in New Mexico in 1947, moved to Oregon in search of better conditions in 1955. Gethsemani made a foundation in 1949 in South Carolina, on a large old plantation donated by Henry R. Luce and Clare Booth Luce. Mepkin is one of the quietest and most beautiful monasteries of the Order. Still small and practically unknown, it moves peacefully along the way of a Cistercian foundation that is not in too big a hurry to become enormous. Another new foundation of Gethsemani was made in the Genessee Valley, New York, in 1951. Our Lady of the Genessee is proving itself to be in many ways a remarkable community which is in every way young, energetic and zealous. The most recent of Gethsemani's foundations was made in California in July, 1955. Our Lady of New Clairvaux is in the Sacramento Valley, on Vina Ranch, a well-known place that has witnessed some important events in the history of northern California since the gold rush. As this book goes to press, news is received that Spencer has made yet another foundation at Snow Mass, Colorado. The other American Trappist monasteries are in Iowa, Georgia, Utah, Missouri and Virginia. A convent of Trappistine nuns has also been founded at Wrentham, Massachusetts.

III

THE HERMIT LIFE

1. *The Carthusians*

Strictly speaking the Carthusians are not and have never been considered a branch of the Benedictine family. St Bruno, the founder of the Grande Chartreuse, spent some time in a priory dependent on the Benedictine Abbey of Molesme, when he was deciding his vocation. But the group which he led into the rugged wilderness of the Alps north of Grenoble were to be hermits in the strict sense of the word, hermits who would bring back to life something of the forgotten purity of the contemplative life as it was once led in the deserts of Egypt.

However, there are several traits in the Carthusian character which bring it, in fact, quite close to the spirit of St Benedict. First of all, the Carthusians, while insisting perhaps more than anyone else in the Western Church upon silence and solitude, have always lived as hermits-in-community. The spokesmen of the Order point out that the Carthusian life combines the advantages of eremitical solitude and of the common life. Lanspergius, for instance, says:

Among the Carthusians you have the two lives, eremitical and cenobitic, so well tempered by the Holy Spirit that whatever might, in either one, have been a danger to you, no longer exists, and we have preserved and increased those elements which foster perfection. Solitude, as it is found in a Charterhouse, is without danger for the monks are not allowed to live according to their whims; they are under the law of obedience and under the direction of their superiors. Although they are alone, they can nevertheless receive assistance and encouragement whenever these become necssary. And yet they are anchorites, so that if they faithfully observe their silence they are in their cells just as if they were in the depths of an uninhabited desert. . . . The solitude of the Carthusians is far more secure than that of the first anchorites, and just as complete.*

Like St Benedict in his Rule, the Carthusians divide their time between manual labor, the chanting of the Divine office, and spiritual reading or study. Finally, their spirit is altogether one with that of St Benedict in its simplicity, its humility and its combination of austerity and discretion.

* Lanspergius, *Enchiridion*, 49.

To say this is simply to say that among the Carthusians we find the same authentic monastic tradition that we find in St Benedict and although there are significant differences of modality between the two orders, no book about Western monasticism would be complete without some mention of the Carthusians.

As a matter of fact the Church has always considered, and has sometimes openly declared, that the Carthusians have been the only monastic order to preserve faithfully the true monastic ideal in all its perfection during centuries in which the other orders fell into decay. The fact that the Carthusians have never needed a reform has long since become proverbial. *Cartusia numquam reformata quia numquam deformata.* "The Charterhouse has never been reformed because it has never been deformed." The enthusiastic praises which Pius XI heaped upon the Order when approving its new constitutions in 1924 are not equalled in any other similar document. The solitary life was termed, by Pope Pius XI, the "most holy form of life," *sanctissimum vitae genus.* And he said of the Carthusians:

It is hardly necessary to say what great hope and expectation the Carthusian monks inspire in us, seeing that since they keep the Rule of their Order not only accurately but also with generous ardor, and since that Rule easily carries those that observe it to the higher degree of sanctity, it is impossible that those religious should not become and remain most powerful pleaders with our most merciful God for all Christendom.*

The Carthusians, then, occupy a place of special eminence among the monastic Orders not only because of the intrinsic perfection of their Rule of life, but also because of the extraordinary fidelity of the Order to that Rule.

What are the special peculiarities of the Carthusian way of life?

While remaining within the traditional monastic framework, the Carthusian life is led almost entirely in the solitude of the monk's cell. The Charterhouse is a compact enough unit to be called a monastery rather than a hermitage. But the monks live, nevertheless, in hermitages. Each cell is in fact a small cottage. The cells are united by a common cloister, and the aspect presented by the average Charterhouse is that of a small, well-ordered village with a church and a block of large buildings at one end, and a series of little roofs huddled around the rectangle of the great cloister. Each cell has its own enclosed garden, and the monk neither sees nor hears what is going on next door. He lives, in fact, all by himself. His cottage is relatively spacious. On the ground floor he has a wood-

---

* Apostolic Constitution *Umbratilem*, July 8, 1924.

shed and a workshop where he exercises his craft, if he has one. There is also a sheltered porch in which he walks when the place is snowed under—which frequently happens, since the Charterhouse is built by preference in the mountains. On the second floor he has, one might be tempted to think, too many rooms. One of them, the *Ave Maria*, is hardly used at all: it is a kind of antechamber to the real cell where the monk spends most of his time. But by a charming and ancient custom, this antechamber, dedicated to the Virgin Mother of God and containing her image, is a place where the monk pauses in prayer on his way in and out of the cell. Carthusian mysticism thinks of the monk's life of solitude as hidden within the Heart of the Virgin Mother.

The real "cell" is a bedroom and sitting room with two alcoves, one an oratory and the other a study. In the one the monk kneels in meditation or recites the day hours of the canonical office with all the ceremonies that are performed when the monks are together in choir. In the other he has his desk, a shelf of books—the Bible, a volume or two of the Fathers, or some theology, some favorite spiritual reading—Ruysbroeck, perhaps, or St John of the Cross, or the Imitation of Christ. And with these one might find almost anything else under the sun if the monk has some special interest, or if he recognizes in himself a need for some light reading. Provided that it is serious and can reasonably be fitted in some way into the monk's life of contemplation, any book may find its way into a Carthusian cell. It is not necessary that the monk confine himself entirely within the limits of conventional piety.

Here, in this central apartment, the monk studies, and meditates, and rests, and takes his meals and recites a good part of the daily office and other appointed prayers.

He usually leaves the cell only three times in twenty-four hours.

First, he rises from a brief four hour sleep about ten-thirty at night, and after some preliminary prayers in his cell he goes to the choir where, with the other monks he chants the long, slow office of Vigils. Pius XI praises the Carthusian choir as he praises everything else about the Order, and he gives us a picture of the monks, chanting in solemn masculine tones, *voce viva et rotunda* without the accompaniment of an organ. Other reports have described the Carthusian chant as having something of the character of a lamentation. Benedictine and Cistercian visitors to the Charterhouse sometimes let fall the remark that "the Carthusians never have any chant practice—it interferes with their solitude" and the implication is that these visitors have found the Carthusian chant not to their liking. Whatever may be the merits of these various views, the Carthusians have always been quite frank in preferring their solitude to everything else, and regarding even the pleasure of beautiful chant as an expendable luxury, if it has to be bought at the price of chant-practices and other distractions of the cenobium.

After the Vigils, which last from two to three hours each night, the Carthusian returns to his cell to complete his night's rest. He will rise and say Prime in his cell in the early morning hours, and then he will again go to Church to sing the conventual Mass. If he is a priest, he will say his own Mass in a chapel attached to the Church and if he is not a priest he will serve Mass and receive Communion. Then he will return again to his cell and spend the rest of his day there until Vespers when, for the last time, he will once again chant the office in choir. This takes place in the middle of the afternoon.

In short, the Carthusian spends nineteen or twenty hours of his day within the limits of his small cottage and garden, seeing no one, speaking to no one, alone with God.

Of course, there may be exceptions. The monk may have an employment or office that obliges him to speak from time to time. He may receive a visitor, occasionally. Once a week there is a three-hour *spatiamentum*—a walk in the country around the Charterhouse, in which everyone must take part. On these walks the monks not only get exercise, but they talk together and the talk, though on a high plane, is not necessarily lugubrious and dull. In other words, it is a necessary break in the monk's solitude. On certain feast days, the monks chant all the day hours in choir together and take their dinner in a common refectory. There is also a sermon preached (in Latin) to the community assembled in chapter.

It is clear that the Carthusian life is notable above all for its single-minded insistence on silence and solitude. All monastic orders recognize that the monk is supposed to live in some sense alone with God. The Carthusians take this obligation as literally as they can. Although they agree with St Benedict that "nothing is to be preferred to the work of God—(the divine office)," they interpret this in a characteristically eremitical fashion. For a long time the Carthusians had no conventual Mass, and the priests of the Order were rarely allowed to say Mass, because the solitude and silence of the cell were regarded as being more important even than Mass. Such an attitude is understood with difficulty today, but we must remember that the Carthusian, even though he may be a priest, is always and primarily a solitary. His chief function in the Church is not to celebrate the liturgical mysteries so much as to live, in silence and alone the mystery of the Church's life "hidden with Christ in God." (Col. 3:3) And in the early days of the Order, when these restrictions were in effect, the idea of "saying Mass" always apparently implied the celebration of Mass with a congregation present.

The spirit of the Carthusians can easily be deduced from the life which they lead. It is a spirit of solitude, silence, simplicity, austerity, aloneness with God. The intransigeance of the Carthusian's flight from the world and from the rest of mankind is meant to purify his heart from all the passions and distractions which necessarily afflict those who are involved in the affairs of the world—or even in the busy, relatively complicated life of a cenobitic monastery. All the legislation which surrounds the Carthusian, and has surrounded him for centuries like an impenetrable wall, is designed to protect his solitude against even those laudable and apparently reasonable enterprises which so often tend to corrupt the purity of the monastic life.

For instance the Carthusians, have always been adamant in refusing dignities and marks of favor and attention from the rest of the Church. While the Benedictines and Cistercians are justly proud of the fact that their Abbots have the pontifical dignity and can celebrate Mass with all the pomp of a bishop, the Carthusians have consistently rejected any such favors. In fact they have refused to allow their houses to be raised to the rank of abbeys, precisely in order to avoid the consequences that might follow.

In order not to attract attention, and to avoid drawing crowds of visitors and postulants, the Carthusians have insisted on keeping their monasteries small and obscure. They have an uncommon distaste for all publicity, and if they are proclaimed as the most perfect of all the Orders in the Church, the proclaiming of the fact is not done by the Carthusians themselves but by others.

The Carthusians have never paid much attention to the apparent sanctity of their members. They have always thought it more important to be saints than to be called saints—another point in which they agree with St Benedict.* Therefore the Carthusians have never taken any steps to procure the canonization of their saints. They do not even have a *Menologium*, or private catalogue of the holiest men of the Order. When a monk of exceptional virtue dies, the highest public honor he receives in the Order is a laconic comment: *laudabiliter vixit*. In good American we would translate this as: "He did

---

* The Carthusians have an adage, "*Non sanctos patefacere sed multos sanctos facere.*" "To make saints, not to publicize them." And St. Benedict tells the monk "not to desire to be called a saint, but to *be* one."

all right." Finally, the Carthusian does not even have the personal distinction of a grave marked with his own name. He is laid away in the cemetery under a plain unmarked cross, and vanishes into anonymity.

The Carthusians have never encouraged any form of work that would bring them back into contact with the outside world. They do not preach retreats, they do not maintain parishes, and when, at times, Carthusians have gained a reputation as spiritual directors, their superiors have intervened to put a stop to it all. The one work of the Carthusian monk that might possibly involve him in fame, is writing. From the beginning the Carthusians have devoted themselves to the copying of manuscripts and the writing of books. Yet here too important qualifications must be made. The greatest writer in the Order, St Bernard's friend the laconic Guigo, was practically the only Carthusian writer for centuries. His "meditations" are mere aphorisms, which can be contained within the pages of a very small volume. Later, writers like Denis de Ryckel, were far less reserved. Yet when one looks into the forty odd volumes of Denis the Carthusian, one gets the impression that with him writing was something like the basket weaving of the early solitaries—a mechanical action that kept him busy and that had no particular reference to an admiring public.

Denis could write a book on any subject, much as a pious housewife might knit a sweater or a pair of socks. One feels that when he had finished a book he was quite indifferent about what happened to it, and would have been just as content to see it burned as to see it printed. This same spirit seems to have guided all the numerous Carthusian writers whose names are on record and whose works have either disappeared or survive only in manuscript. They are unknown, they are never read and the reason is that they did not really write to be read. They worked like the Desert Father in Cassian who, at the end of each year, used to burn all the baskets he had woven and start over again. Today, if a Carthusian writes something for publication, it never appears under any name.

In short, the Carthusians have never thought that the perfection of the spiritual life and true purity of heart could be preserved merely by what is called the "practice of interior solitude." The ancient Customs of the Order, the *Consuetudines* written in the 12th century by Prior Guigo of the Grande Chartreuse, end with a beautiful panegyric on solitude—physical solitude.* Here we read that nowhere better than in true solitude does the monk discover the hidden sweetness of the psalms, the value of study

---

* Consuetudines Guigonis, c.80, P.L. 153:758.

and reading, intense fervor in prayer, the delicate sense of spiritual realities in meditation, the
ecstasy of contemplation and the purifying tears
of compunction. The purpose of Carthusian
solitude is found in these words and in their
context. Like every other monk, the Carthusian
is the son and follower of the ancient prophets,
of Moses and Elias, of John the Baptist, of Jesus
Himself who fasted in the desert and spent
many nights alone on the mountain in prayer.
The purpose of Carthusian solitude is to place
the soul in a state of silence and receptivity that
will open its spiritual depths to the action of
the Holy Spirit who makes known the mysteries of the Kingdom of God and teaches us
the unsearchable riches of the love and the wisdom of Christ.

Commenting on this chapter of Guigo, Dom
Innocent Lemasson summarizes it and defines
the Carthusian spirit in the following terms:

The principles of the Carthusian life are *quiet*
(quies) or rest from worldly things and desires,
solitude which removes us from the company of
men and from the sight of vanities, *silence* from
useless speaking, and the *quest for supernal realities*
(superiorum appetitio) that is to say seeking and
delighting in the things that are above. All other
matters are passed over (by Guigo in this text) because he considers them accidental to the true sub-

stance of the Carthusian vocation which is obedience, offered up in quiet, in silence and in solitude.*

From the very beginning the Carthusians
realized that this vocation was a very uncommon one and that the Carthusian life would
never be popular or well understood. In the
same commentary just quoted, Dom Lemasson
remarks that God alone can make monks and
hermits, and that human expedients to increase
the number of Carthusian vocations would only
end in the ruin of the Order. The Carthusians
have, in fact, always been the most exacting of
all Orders in their admission of candidates, on
the ground that "many are called to the faith
but very few are foreordained to become Carthusians." ** As a result they may have seemed
extremely exclusive and snobbish, in comparison
to other Orders, but in fact the great prudence
which they have always exercised in this matter
of vocations has been one of the chief reasons
why the Order has never needed a reform.

If we pause a moment to look a little more
closely at this singular grace of the Carthusians,
we will see that it cannot be explained merely
by fidelity to their Constitutions and to the
principles of their founders. It is true that the
Carthusians have been exceptionally loyal to

---

* Commentary on the Consuetudines, c.80, P.L. 153:756.
** Dom Lemasson, loc. cit. col. 759.

their traditional ideal. But mere fidelity to a Rule can itself end by distorting and eventually destroying the life for which the Rule was written, unless it is constantly supported by the interior spirit by which the rule was inspired.

The Carthusians have been preserved not only by their rigid exterior discipline, but by the inner flexibility which has accompanied it. They have been saved not merely by human will clinging firmly to a Law, but above all by the humility of hearts that abandoned themselves to the Spirit Who dictated the Law. Looking at the Carthusians from the outside, one might be tempted to imagine them proud. But when one knows a little more about them and their life, one understands that only a very humble man could stand Carthusian solitude without going crazy. For the solitude of the Charterhouse will always have a devastating effect on pride that seeks to be alone with itself. Such pride will crumble into schizophrenia in the uninterrupted silence of the cell. It is in any case true that the great temptation of all solitaries is something much worse than pride—it is the madness that lies beyond pride, and the solitary must know how to keep his balance and his sense of humor. Only humility can give him that peace. Strong with the strength of Christ's humility, which is at the same time Christ's truth, the monk can face his solitude without supporting himself by unconsciously magical or illuministic habits of mind. In other words, he can bear the purification of solitude which slowly and inexorably separates faith from illusion. He can sustain the dreadful searching of soul that strips him of his vanities and self-deceptions, and he can peacefully accept the fact that when his false ideas of himself are gone he has practically nothing else left. But then he is ready for the encounter with reality: the Truth and the Holiness of God, which he must learn to confront in the depths of his own nothingness.

What one finds in the Charterhouse, then, is not a collection of great mystics and men of dazzling spiritual gifts, but simple and rugged souls whose mysticism is all swallowed up in a faith too big and too simple for visions. The more spectacular gifts have been left for lesser spirits, who move in the world of action.

When the Carthusians landed in America for the first time in 1951, it could be said that the Church in the United States had finally come of age. The Carthusian foundation at Whitingham, Vermont, is still in the experimental stage: but it is a stage of such primitive simplicity that one feels the founders will look back to it with great happiness in years to come.

There is as yet no real Charterhouse at Whitingham. There is a lonely farmhouse, "Sky Farm" is what it is called, and this accommodates guests and postulants. Further back in the woods are a group of shanties—four of them in all. These are the cells. They are built on the probable site of the future Charterhouse, and have none of the elaborateness and self-contained security of the true Carthusian cottage. Here the hermits live in peace, keeping the austere Carthusian rule with only those modifications demanded by the provisional nature of their dwelling. Meanwhile postulants present themselves from time to time, are tested for a few months, then sent to Europe for their novitiate. In the last four years, practically all those chosen have failed to meet the requirements of the Order or sustain the hardships of fasting, cold, and solitude in the frozen silence of an Alpine winter. But here and there a survivor makes his vows and becomes a professed Carthusian. The cornerstone of the American community is one of the founders of Whitingham, a former Benedictine who taught psychiatry at the Catholic University in Washington. Dom Thomas Verner Moore left Washington for Spain in 1948, and was received as a novice at the Spanish Charterhouse of Miraflores, near Burgos, and he has undoubtedly been one of the guiding spirits in the American foundation.

The Charterhouse in America will have to

meet the great temptations which this country offers to all the monastic orders—publicity, technology, popularity, commercialism, machines and the awful impulsion to throw everything overboard for the sake of fame and prosperity (masking as an "apostolate of example"). One feels that the Carthusians are equipped, as no other Order, to resist this attack of the world upon the monastic spirit. The whole monastic structure in America may eventually depend on their doing so successfully.

2. The Camaldolese

All that has been said in these pages points to the fact that the monastic life is above all a life of deep spiritual peace and fruitfulness, which gives us, even on earth, a foretaste of the peace of heaven. But we have also come to understand that the peace of the monastic life is not a material peace, not a state of comfortable inertia, guaranteed by the absence of all cares and responsibilities. Concerning a peace which gratifies the body rather than the soul, Christ said only that He came to bring "not peace but the sword" (Matt. 10:34). The peace of the monk is proportionate to his detachment from the things of earth. It is the peace not of one who finds all his earthly desires and needs taken care of in a satisfactory manner, but of one who, to some extent, has become independent of material things by concentrating his whole life on a search for the Kingdom of God. He is free, with the liberty of the sons of God. His peace is not of this world. It is hidden with Christ in God.

The monastic life is the more hidden in proportion as it is humble, solitary and poor. The monastic spirit is above all a spirit of solitude, of separation from the world. The hermit is by nature alienated from the apostolic ministry of preaching, as well as from prelacies and dignities that would keep him before the eyes of men. If he is, like the Apostles, a "spectacle to angels and to men" it can only be as an example of poverty from which the world tends to turn away without understanding. Consequently, every monk has in his heart the aspiration for an ever greater solitude, and poverty and humility. If the dispositions of divine Providence may involve him, for a time, in work that places him before the public, he knows that this disposition is purely accidental, and that the essence of his vocation remains the same: it is always a call to solitude, to self-renunciation. It is a call to the desert.

St Benedict, in his profound wisdom, realized that all men could not follow his example and pass immediately from the turbulent cities to the rocky valleys of the wilderness. Not all men are capable of living alone in caves. And it is not necessary to live in a cleft of the rocks to become a monastic saint. In writing a rule for cenobites, in which all the emphasis is placed on humility and obedience, and in which the spirit of the desert is maintained and made accessible to all, St Benedict succeeded in transplanting the monastic ideal of the Egyptian desert to European soil. Not only that, but he ensured the permanent survival of the desert ideal. He was only able to do so by tempering some of the austerities of the hermits of the Thebaid, and prudently softening the rigors of Pachomian cenobitism. The Benedictine monastery is essentially a family rather than a military camp, although Benedict himself is not afraid to use an occasional martial metaphor.

But we must never suppose, as is sometimes supposed, that in prudently adapting the observances of the Egyptian monks to European needs, St Benedict was in any way repudiating the primitive monastic ideal. On the contrary, the *raison d'etre* of his adaptation is to be sought in the ideal itself which he sought to preserve.

The Rule of St Benedict, which so often quotes verbatim from the monastic traditions of the East, and which relies so heavily on Cassian, the popularizer of Oriental monachism, is written for monks who are to live in the direct line of the pure, ancient tradition. The monk who vows obedience under the Rule of St Benedict is therefore the true descendent of St Anthony of the desert as well as of St Pachomius and of St Basil. He enters upon the monastic life as a cenobite, indeed: but there is nothing in the very nature of his vocation itself to exclude a deep admiration for the ancient hermits, or to prevent his desiring to share something of their solitary contemplation of God. On the contrary, if the monk were to sever all the spiritual bonds which tie him to the Desert Fathers, he would be cutting himself off from the purest original source of his monastic spirit. He would be depriving himself of the substantial nourishment which St Benedict himself saw to be necessary for his soul. But for this nourishment to profit his soul he must do what was done by St Benedict himself, and distinguish the essentials of the monastic life (the spirit of self-renunciation to seek God) from the accidentals (extraordinary bodily mortifications and the practice of extreme asceticism).

The fact that St Benedict considers the cenobites to be the "strongest breed" (*fortissimum genus*) among monks, does not mean that he either excludes or underestimates the anchorites. On the contrary, as a representative of the authentic tradition in this matter, he takes it for granted that some monks, after long testing in the cenobium, will want to go off into solitude and will receive permission to do so. This implicit orientation of the Rule of St Benedict towards eremitical solitude, which is so often denied or underestimated, brings us to the point where we must consider, in greater detail, the eremitical branch of the Benedictine family.

One of the most venerable and ancient shoots of the primitive Benedictine stock is the Order of Camaldoli. This Order explicitly takes upon itself the task of providing a refuge for the pure contemplative life, in solitude. Born of the intense revival of monastic fervor that swept Europe in the tenth and eleventh centuries, Camaldoli was founded in a high valley of the Appenines, beyond Arrezzo, by St Romuald in 1012. Entirely unique in western monasticism of the present day, the Camaldolese hermitage presents the aspect of an ancient *laura*—a village of detached cells, clustered around the Church. Unlike the typical Charterhouse, whose cells are all next to one another and open out on a common cloister, Camaldoli jealously insists on the fact that the cells must be separate from one another at least by a distance of twenty or thirty feet. The hermits live, read, work, eat, sleep and meditate in their cells, but gather for the canonical hours in the Church. Silence and solitude, essential to the true life of contemplation, are here not a mere question of "spirit" and of "ideal" but also belong to the letter of the rule. For Camaldoli, like the Chartreuse, realizes that "interior silence" and "interior solitude" do not suffice, by themselves, to guarantee a purely contemplative life. Interior silence may well be the refuge of the monk engaged in a more or less active life, who seeks God in moments of recollection. But the best way to foster interior silence is to preserve exterior silence, and the best way to have interior solitude is not to be alone in a crowd but to be simply and purely alone.

The purpose of this solitude is to enable the monk to live alone with God in an atmosphere which is most propitious for deep interior prayer. There has never been any question, in Christian tradition, of the fact that the most propitious atmosphere for real contemplation is the solitude of a hermit's cell. Corporate and liturgical prayer are indeed important in the life of the Church and of the monk but they do not of themselves satisfy the deep need for intimate contact with God in solitary prayer, a need which constitutes the peculiar vocation of the contemplative soul. Liturgical prayer re-

motely, disposes us for the grace of contemplation. And this gift of God, like all other gifts
of God, is granted to souls as an outpouring of
the infinite riches of God given to us, in Christ,
in the Holy Sacrifice of the Mass. But the true
fruition of this special gift is not usually possible unless our Eucharistic communion is some-
how prolonged in silent and solitary adoration.
The hermit's whole life is a life of silent adoration. His very solitude keeps him ever in the
presence of God, if he is faithful to the grace of
his hidden state. His whole day, in the silence of
his cell, or of his garden looking out upon the
forest, is a prolonged Communion. Even in the
old days when communion was less frequent,
the life of the hermit could hardly help being
anything but Eucharistic in the broad sense of
a life of praise and thanksgiving for the gifts of
God—a life nourished by the constant awareness of the great reality of God and of His
action in the world, in Christ.

St Peter Damian, whom Camaldoli rightly
claims as one of her great spokesmen and wit-
nesses, was profoundly aware of the hermit's
place in the unity of the Mystical Christ. Indeed, he says, that the unity of the Church, in
which all the souls of the faithful are fused into
one Being by the fire of divine charity, is also
present in each individual soul, so that wherever

a member of Christ is present, the whole Christ is present in him.

The Church of Christ is so connected in its members, united by charity with one another, that in many she is one, and in each individual she is mysteriously present as a whole. Thus the whole Church is rightly called one Spouse of Christ, and each single soul, by virtue of the mystery of this sacrament, is rightly believed to be the whole Church.*

The saint illustrates this by comparing the unity of Christ in His Mystical Body with his unity in His sacramental Body. Just as on all the altars of the world there is but one Body of Christ, and one chalice of His Most Precious Blood, so the whole Christ is present in each individual member of the Church. It is by virtue of these principles that St Peter Damian shows how the hermit priest, reciting the office alone in his mountain oratory, can and indeed must say "Dominus vobiscum" and answer himself "Et cum spiritu tuo." The whole Church is present in the cell where he is alone.

The fact that this mystical integration in the whole Christ is increased by solitude is the theological justification for the eremitical life. And the joy of the hermit in his vocation of pure solitude and renunciation is a river which goes

---

* *Liber qui dicitur Dominus Vobiscum,* c.5.

forth, through the secret channels of the communion of saints, to make glad the city of God and strengthen the arms of those who labor and fight for God in the market places of the distant cities. This heightened sense of unity in Christ is also the source of the hermit's "Eucharistic" spirit and the fountain head of his thanksgiving. Even though in his solitude he may have moments of terrible darkness and isolation, even though his sense of his own poverty and aloneness before God may grow as the years go on, the hermit never loses his deep sense of supernatural solidarity with the whole Mystical Body of Christ. Why should he? Unlike the Apostle, who is often bewildered and blinded by the confusion that surrounds him at all times, the hermit may, by the gift of God, come to a deep realization of the fact that he is present by his prayers and by his charity in the hearts of men whom he will never see on earth. He will be obscurely reassured of the fruitfulness of his hidden apostolate which is all the more effective for being uniquely and integrally supernatural— a pure product of theological virtue, and of prayer directed by the Holy Ghost.

One of the peculiar characteristics of Camaldoli is the fact that the Camaldolese hermit may even receive permission to become a recluse. After five years of solemn profession, a hermit who is well qualified and tested may receive per-

mission to live absolutely alone and undisturbed
in his cell, never coming out to join the others
in the Church or in their common gatherings
except three times a year: on St Martin's Day
(in November) and on Quinquagesima Sunday, days of recreation which precede the two
monastic Lents, and during the last three days
of Holy Week. At all other times, the recluses
remain in the cell and their walled garden, say
Mass in their own private oratory if they are
priests, and never communicate with the other
hermits either by the spoken word or by writing, except with special permission. When they
hear the bells for the canonical hours, they recite them in their cells, and in addition to the
prayers said by the others they also recite fifty
psalms, and devote twice as much time to meditation. But on the whole the number of prescribed prayers and practices are not increased,
since it is assumed that the recluse, being a
mature, solitary and capable of responding to
the inspirations of divine grace by himself, will
abandon himself to the guidance of the Holy
Spirit in a life of holy freedom, subject of
course to the control of a wise director, and in
obedience to the Prior.

The singular advantage of such a life is that
it makes it possible for a pure contemplative
life of real solitude and simplicity, without for-
malism and without rigid, inflexible prescrip-

tions of minor detail, yet fully protected by spiritual control and by religious obedience. The hermit and the recluse, being true sons of St Benedict and living under an authentic interpretation of his Holy Rule, are never exempted in principle from the obedience which keeps them in direct contact with the sanctifying and formative action exercised by Christ through the hierarchy of His Church. Union with the visible representatives of Christ only strengthens and protects the inner spiritual action of the Holy Spirit Who carries on His secret work in the soul of the hermit all the more freely because obedience has removed the obstacles to His action. The Prior, on the other hand, himself a hermit and a man of God, knows how to exercise his authority in such a way as to encourage the free response of each soul to its own individual call.

The founders of Camaldoli, and St Peter Danian, are sometimes taxed with an excessive severity which goes far beyond the limits of Benedictine discretion. It is true that the first hermits of Camaldoli sought to reproduce, in their hidden cells, more than the solitude and contemplation of the desert fathers. They were great lovers of austerity, and the energy with which they practiced bodily penance may seem, to us, to have been inordinately violent. It was an energy characteristic of those times. Yet its excessive rigor is not essential to the Camaldolese way of life.

In order to evaluate the true spirit of Camaldoli, we must look not only at the writings of St Peter Damian or the life of St Romuald, but also and above all that the Constitutions, written by Blessed Rudolf, which alone can give a true well-rounded picture of the Camaldolese life and its spirit.

Here we see, first of all, an observance that is austere but not extreme. It is marked, on the contrary, by a spirit of remarkable discretion and breadth of view. In an age which produced many monuments of monastic legislation, this is one of the most admirable documents as well as one of the least known. It certainly merits to rank with the Consuetudines of Guigo the Carthusian or the Usages of Cîteaux. Earlier than both of these, it is less strictly juridicial in its tone. Many of the chapters are purely ascetic. Others are theological. The effect of the whole is one of balance and sanity and supernatural good sense. It reflects at once the true spirit of the Gospel of Christ, and the wisdom of the greatest Desert Fathers who, far from being extremists, were remarkable above all for their prudence in singular contrast to the intemperate zeal of their lesser contemporaries.

The Constitutions of Blessed Rudolf provide not only for the hermitage of Camaldoli, but also for a monastery of cenobites, which is to be nearby and to act as a point of contact with the outside world. The Camaldolese still preserve this combination of cenobitical and eremitical communities. The Monastery of cenobites receives and trains novices for the hermitage. It takes care of guests, it feeds the poor. It supplies food and other needs for the hermitage, and it receives the hermits when they are sick and need medical care. It must not be thought, however, that the Camaldolese have a divided vocation, a life in which one may be either a hermit or a cenobite by choice. The monastery of cenobites serves a useful purpose and there must of necessity be some monks there to keep it going and do the work that it involves. But at Camaldoli one is only a cenobite by accidental necessity, and a hermit by choice. The solitary life is the true essence of the vocation, and no one is supposed to remain for more than three consecutive years out of the hermitage.

The hermitage, at the same time, has all the major advantages of the common life. Above all, it is founded on a solid juridical foundation which protects the hermit against the instability of human nature, providing him with guidance and support, without interfering with the freedom of spirit without which the truly contemplative life could not possibly develop. At the same time, the framework of customs and of monastic obedience remains nothing more than a framework. Within this frame, the hermit himself must take his life in hand, and manfully accomplish in silence and in solitude the work which God has destined for him. This cannot possibly be done without great energy, persevering courage, profound faith, and real spiritual maturity. When St Benedict called cenobitism the "strongest" division of the monastic family, he meant that cenobitism was strongest as an *institution* and that its members could find a peculiar strength and support in the presence and life of their community. Ideally speaking, the eremitical life is in no sense an institution. It is a life lived alone with God, under the light and the guidance of God alone. Camaldoli, true to the spirit of St Benedict, makes this extraordinary ideal more accessible by giving at least the essentials of an institutional set-up. But in the last analysis the strength of the hermit is not to be sought in any rule or any obedience or any guidance imposed on him from the outside. He has to be one of those rare men who is strong with an inner spiritual consistency that is all his own and which enables him to function in solitude, without the stimulus of example or the fear of criticism. It is not simple for a man to live constantly on a high level of integrity when he is seen by no one except God. It requires both great faith and an unusual strength of character.

The Camaldolese hermit can count on this interior strength, however, for he belongs to the great Benedictine family, and is formed by the spirit and the living tradition of the greatest of monks. Hence his life is simple and strong, and it has deep roots in the wisdom of the Church. One even feels that the primitive austerity of Camaldolese solitude would greatly appeal to St Benedict if he were alive today. It is probably not exaggerated to say that the Father of western monks would feel himself more at home in the simple mountain hermitage than in many a greater and more splendid monastery amid the cities of the plain.

In all religious life, the spirit is vastly more important than the letter. But the more solitary a life becomes, the more important is its spirit and the less important the letter of the rule. The eremitical life is almost exclusively spirit. That is why the letter of its legislation is generally extremely simple. The early customs of Camaldoli, to which we have already referred, are no exception. That is why they are extremely adaptable to all places (provided they be solitary places) and to all times. The accidentals appear clearly for what thy are, and one easily sees that nothing essential to the life is lost, for instance, by a diminution of the great quantity of vocal prayers that were said in the early days, a mitigation of the extreme fasting, and a discreet moderation of the almost continual scourging that was practiced in the eleventh century.

The main purpose of the Camaldolese life is union with God by solitary prayer in the silence of the cell. Everything is directed to this end. All that the hermit does should promote that *puritas cordis* which makes contemplative union possible. The two great means to this end are silence and meditation. Both, says Bl. Rudolf, are vitally important. Neither one is of any avail without the other. "For silence without meditation is death, it is like a man buried alive. But meditation without silence is pure frustration—it is like the struggling of the man buried alive, in his sepulchre. But both silence and meditation together bring great rest to the soul and lead it to perfect contemplation." *

The silence that is required for this interior meditation is first of all a silence of the tongue, a silence of the body, a silence of the heart. The tongue renounces useless and evil speaking. The body is silent when it abandons useless and harmful actions. The heart is silent when it is purified from useless and evil thoughts. For what would be the use of keeping silence with your tongue, if you have tumult of vices raising

---

* Constitutiones, c.44.

a storm in your actions and in your mind? The purpose of this silence is not merely negative. It has a positive and constructive force in the life of prayer. It is indeed one of the best and most efficacious of ascetic weapons because it is one of the most positive. Silence builds the life of prayer which, like the Temple of Solomon, is an edifice which must grow without the sound of any iron tool. "The house of God grows in sacred silence, and a temple that will never fall is constructed without noises." And the legislator goes on: "If you are quiet and humble, you will not fear what your flesh may do to you. For where the Heavenly Dweller rests in peace, the betrayer cannot prevail." It is in the silent soul that wisdom takes up her abode, and remains forever. (*In silenti, et quiescenti vel meditanti anima permanet sapientia.*) *

Just as St Anthony of the Desert placed discretion at the top of his list of virtues, as being the mother of them all, so too the Camaldolese hermit will learn to live in a spirit of sobriety and moderation. The *sobrietas* we here consider is too big to be fitted into the narrow limits of a scholastic category. It overflows the bounds of temperance and includes prudence and justice and fortitude. Like Benedictine humility, it is really an integrated organism of good habits

---

* Constitutiones, 44.

which governs and orders all our actions in reference to their proper end. The sobriety of the Camaldolese hermit therefore not only moderates his bodily appetites, but restrains the appetites of his soul and leads him in all things along a path of simplicity and wisdom. In fact, sobriety not only curbs gluttony, but also restrains the inordinate zeal for fasting. It not only teaches us to keep silence, but teaches us to speak at the right time. It not only spurs us on to courageous vigils and night prayers, but also tempers our zeal for penance and tells us when we ought to sleep. In succinct words, sobriety is a virtue by which we "curb the passions of the flesh, but do not destroy our nature." "For we must kill the carnal desires when they fight against our soul, but we must not destroy the sense organs which are useful to the soul. But living soberly, and piously, and justly in this world, we will, by sobriety, provide for ourselves, and by justice we will come to the help of our neighbor, and by piety we will serve God." *

This mention of care for one's neighbor reminds us that fraternal charity is by no means excluded from the eremitical life. It cannot be, and St Basil's accusation that the hermit has no opportunity to practice this all important virtue

---

* Constitutiones, 41.

is not altogether exact. The hermit has always recognized his obligation towards his neighbor —which is not only an obligation to pray for others, but also to perform corporal and spiritual works of mercy at certain times.

This brings us back to the existence of the *cenobium*, the monastery traditionally attached to the hermitage. Chapter 38 of the *Constitutiones* considers it reasonable that each hermit should desire to take his turn in the active life of serving the poor and the sick and entertaining the guests. Here too sobriety is in command. It would be wrong for him to desire too much activity, but it would also be wrong for him not to desire any activity at all. On the contrary, a certain amount of moderate activity will make his solitary life more fruitful and enable him to return to his prayer with a relaxed mind and a renewed enthusiasm for the interior life.

The exterior activity of charity of which we speak here is directed to guests from the world outside and is of course quite different from the ordinary manual or intellectual labor which the hermit daily performs in his own cell. It is also different from the normal amount of service which the hermit performs when he takes his part in the simplified routine of communal life and prayer that still exists in the hermitage-community. It is clear, then, that the Camaldolese hermit does not live in absolute isolation and that he does have plentiful opportunities for the exercise of charity, without being overwhelmed with exterior duties and activities.

The *Constitutiones* stress the fact that human feeling, supernaturalized by a spirit of mercy and compassion, is most necessary for hermits: *Pietas solitariis* valde *necessaria est.** They must be kind, meek, gentle, humane. The reason for the emphasis placed on this virtue is, of course, that the professional hazard of solitude is precisely a growing insensibility to human values. This is by all means to be considered a hazard, not as a virtue. It is not recommended that the solitary become merely "tough." On the contrary, if his heart becomes hardened, the road to sanctity will be barred before him. The narrow gate is not opened to men without human sympathy, and incapable of supernatural affection.

Pietas [says our author] is a kind disposition of heart which, with merciful tenderness, is patient and sympathizes with the weaknesses of other men. For solitaries often show themselves unduly austere and unkind to others under the pretext of eremitical severity, as though they themselves were not like everyone else.

The training ground in which this virtue is practiced and acquired is, once again, the rudi-

---

* Constitutiones, 42.

mentary community life that still exists among the hermits of Camaldoli. Kindness is not learned without contact with human weakness, and even in the hermitage it is obligatory, above all, to practice that charity which is the fullfillment of the whole Law. There is no Christian perfection without sharing in the tender sympathy and patience which the Saviour of the world showed towards the weak, the un-gifted, the unloved, and the unfortunate sinner.

Nevertheless, though these virtues have to be stressed in the life of the solitary because they are inseparable from the very vocation of a Christian, they are not the peculiar essence of his vocation. The special call of the hermit is always to solitude and contemplation, and by far the greater part of his time is spent in the cell where he has no opportunity to practice these other works of virtue. Patience and stability in the silence of his cell are the most important and most fundamental of his specific virtues, along with the silence and meditation without which his cell would be nothing but a tomb. Indeed, when a solitary loses the true spirit of his vocation, his cell is no longer able to contain him. It casts him out, as the sea casts up a dead body on the shore.*

Hence the importance of constant and fruit-

* Consuetudines, 36.

ful occupation. This occupation should be, by preference, interior and spiritual, and should not require a great amount of moving around. Time is spent of course in house-cleaning and gardening, for each cell has a somewhat large garden enclosed within its wall, and the *Constitutiones* speak of the hermits going out into the forest to cut and gather firewood. At the present day the hermits of Camaldoli also gather herbs and resins in the forest in order to distill a liqueur, the sale of which contributes to their support. The chief occupations of the solitary in his cell, besides meditative prayer, are reading, study, recitation of the Psalms, and other simple occupations which are not incompatible with the solitary life such as writing or drawing, the making of rosaries or the exercise of some craft. The more spiritual occupations are preferred because they do not disturb the "tranquillity of the hermitage" with undue agitation, but on the whole some latitude is allowed, and the spirit of the Camaldolese life is supple and flexible, so as not to paralyze the action of the Spirit or to crush human weakness by a too rigid confinement.

When this spirit is acquired and fully lived, it brings a joy that has no comparison anywhere on earth. "To the quiet and persevering hermit, his sojourn in the cell brings a refreshing sweetness and a blessed silence which seem to be a taste of paradise." *

Of all the Orders described in this volume, the Camaldolese are numerically the smallest. One still looks in vain for a foundation of Camaldolese hermits in North America. Fifty years ago there was one in Brazil, but it no longer exists.

The Camaldolese are divided into two groups, one of which maintains both hermitages and cenobitic monasteries, the other of which clings exclusively to the hermit life and has no *cenobium*. The former congregation has its seat at Camaldoli itself, and is called the "Hermit-Monks of Camaldoli." It has monasteries and hermitages in various parts of Italy. The second group, called the "Camaldolese Hermits of Monte Corona," has hermitages in Italy, Spain and Poland.

Until recently there was also a Camaldolese hermitage in southern France but this was closed down before the Second World War. Since then it has been taken over by the Discalced Carmelite Friars, who have revived their ancient custom of setting aside solitary places as "deserts" or hermitages for periodic retreats into solitude. Here the friars may withdraw for a few months or a year and renew in solitude the contact with God that is so essential for a fruitful apostolate.

The world of men has forgotten the joys of

---

* Constitutiones, 36.

silence, the peace of solitude which is necessary, to some extent, for the fullness of human living. Not all men are called to be hermits, but all men need enough silence and solitude in their lives to enable the deep inner voice of their own true self to be heard at least occasionally. When that inner voice is not heard, when man cannot attain to the spiritual peace that comes from being perfectly at one with his own true self, his life is always miserable and exhausting. For he cannot go on happily for long unless he is in contact with the springs of spiritual life which are hidden in the depths of his own soul. If man is constantly exiled from his own home, locked out of his own spiritual solitude, he ceases to be a true person. He no longer lives as a man. He is not even a healthy animal. He becomes a kind of automaton, living without joy because he has lost all spontaneity. He is no longer moved from within, but only from outside himself. He no longer makes decisions for himself, he lets them be made for him. He no longer acts upon the outside world, but lets it act upon him. He is propelled through life by a series of collisions with outside forces. His is no longer the life of a human being, but the existence of a sentient billiard ball, a being without purpose and without any deeply valid response to reality.

The serene and sober beauty of the monastic ideal, and particularly the austere simplicity and joy of contemplative solitude, are often pointed to as a condemning contrast to the world of sin. And this is true. The humility of the monk is indeed a reproach to the insolent self-sufficiency of modern man, whether he be a totalitarian or a capitalist. The povery and self-denial of the monk, his meekness, his obedience, his solitude, condemn the insatiable greed, the pitiful lack of self-control, the craven dependence of man who is left at the mercy of modern society.

But in proposing to the world the sanctity of the monastic life as an example, the Church does not merely seek to humiliate and reproach sinners. In fact, that is never her attitude. She is a kind mother. Her authority seeks to develop men to help them grow and seek happiness, not merely to punish them and reprove them and take away even the last ounces of vitality and joy which they still retain in their souls. The monastic life is therefore always a witness to the joy and vitality and fruitfulness of the life of the Church. It is in this sense above all that monasticism will always manifest the Church's inexhaustible reservoirs of sanctity. For sanctity and life are one: holiness is the special value of the life that comes to man's soul direct from God. Holiness is life lived in its fullness, in union with the Living God. Life brings to perfection all the deepest resources of man's nature, before elevating him to the perfection of supernatural and mystical union.

The Desert Fathers knew this well. One of

them, Abbot Isaias, expounds the traditional doctrine of the Fathers: that man, made in the image of God, was made for perfect union with Him. Having lost the capacity for union by Adam's sin, he had recovered it in Christ. Through Christ man returns to the original perfection intended for human nature by God. The Christian life is therefore a return to "paradise," a partial restoration of the joy and peace of Adam's contemplative life in Eden. In saving man, the passion of Christ has also healed his body and all its faculties, and indeed the sanctifying power of the Cross has poured itself out upon the whole world, and man is once again able to find God in himself and in everything else. This Patristic doctrine is the basis for all we have seen in our consideration of the monastic way of life. Here is what Abbot Isaias says:

I would not have you ignorant, brethren, that when God made man in the beginning he placed him in paradise with all the faculties of his soul in perfect order and according to his nature. But after man had listened to the deceiver, all his faculties were turned against his nature, and he was cast down from his proper dignity. But Our Lord, driven by His great charity, declared His mercy to mankind. The Word was made flesh, that is to say He was made a perfect man, like unto us in all things except sin, in order that by His holy Body He might call us back to the original perfection of our nature. For showing man His mercy He led man back into paradise. . . . He has given us a holy way of serving God and a pure law, that man might be brought back into that state of nature in which he was created by God.*

This "return to paradise," this return to the perfection of charity in which man was created by God, is the true end of the monastic life. And in all the great Rules, and all the traditional documents of the great monks of the past, this return is seen as an ascent to divine contemplation. Just as Moses in the solitude of Mount Horeb led his flocks into the inner parts of the desert, and there saw the burning bush, and heard the Voice that spoke, and learned, from the Voice, the unutterable and Holy Name of God, so too the monk penetrates into the wilderness by silence and perfect solitude. There he discovers the "burning bush" which is his own spirit, enkindled with the fire of God but not consumed. In order to contemplate this tremendous mystery he must imitate Moses and remove his "shoes"—that is to say, he must rise above all conceptions of God: for the God he is approaching is a mere "object" able to be contained within the limits of a concept. He is the Living God, burning like an intangible flame within the substance of our own spirit that derives all its life from Him. He is not experienced except by the soul that burns with His Flame.

---

* Oratio XI, *De Mente secundum naturam.*

The Flame of God is the Flame of pure life, infinite Being, Absolute Reality. Only those know Him who have themselves abandoned all falsity and all illusion and all pretense and all sham. More than that, they have abandoned themselves, they have ascended above themselves, they are beyond themselves. And in rising beyond themselves, they have become most perfectly themselves, no longer in themselves but in Him.

The voice they hear is no longer the voice of a philosophical intuition, no longer the echo of the words of divine revelation, but the very substance of reality itself—Realty not as a concept, but as a Person.

And thou, whoever thou art, who livest in solitude, and leadest a solitary life having led thy flocks, that is to say thy simple thoughts and thy humble affections, into the depths of thy loving will, there thou wilt find the bush of thy humility, which heretofore brought forth nothing but thorns and briars, radiant with the light of God. For thou wilt be glorifying and bearing God in thy own body. This is the divine fire which enlightens us without burning us, gives radiance but does not consume us . . . And the bush that burns without being consumed is human nature enkindled with the fire of divine love, and unharmed by the slightest touch of destruction.*

---

* B. *Rudolfi Constitutiones,* c.1.

EPILOGUE

The Monk and the World

The monastery is neither a museum nor an asylum. The monk remains in the world from which he has fled, and he remains a potent, though hidden, force in that world. Beyond all the works which may accidentally attach themselves to his vocation, the monk acts on the world simply by being a monk. The presence of contemplatives is, to the world, what the presence of yeast is to dough for, twenty centuries ago, Christ Himself made clear that the Kingdom of Heaven is like yeast hidden in three measures of meal.

Even though he may never leave his monastery, never speak a word to the rest of men, the monk is inextricably involved in the common suffering and problems of the society in which he lives. He cannot escape from them, nor does he desire to. He is not exempted from service in fighting the great battles of his age, but rather, as a soldier of Christ, he is appointed to fight these battles on a spiritual front, in mystery, by self-sacrifice and prayer. He does this, united with Christ on the Cross, united to all those for whom Christ died, and conscious that his battle is not against flesh and blood "but against principalities and powers, against the rulers of the world of this darkness, against the spirits of wickedness in the high places." (Ephesians, 6:12)

The world of our time is in confusion. It is reaching the peak of the greatest crisis in history. Never before has there been such a total upheaval of the whole human race. Tremendous forces are at work, spiritual, sociological, economic, technological and least of all political. Mankind stands on the brink of a new barbarism, yet at the same time there remain possibilities for an unexpected and almost unbelievable solution, the creation of a new world and a new civilization the like of which has never been seen. We are face to face either with Antichrist or the Millennium, no one knows which.

In this changing world, the monk remains as the bulwark of an unchanging Church against which the gates of hell cannot prevail. True, the Church herself changes, because she is a living Body, a growing organism. Where there is life, there must be change. The monastic Order too, must change, develop, grow.

Before God, before man, before the world of

concupiscence which is his antagonist, the monk stands burdened with a tremendous responsibility to go on being what he is called, a monk, a man of God, and not only one who has fled the world, but who is capable of representing God in the world which the Son of God has saved by His death on the Cross.

The monastery can never be merely the refuge of fake gothic architecture, classical learning and conventional piety. If the monk is nothing more than a well established bourgeois, with comfortable middle class prejudices and all the usual blind spots, he will find that his life has been dedicated not to God but to the "service of corruption," but he will vanish with all that is evanescent.

On the other hand, his vocation prohibits him from descending into the plain and joining in the battles that go on there. The choices that the world offers him, the chances to align himself with one side or another, can only be regarded as temptations. His vocation calls him exclusively to the transcendent. He is, and must always remain, above every human faction. That means that he is likely to become the victim of every one of them. He should not renounce his exclusively spiritual position in order to protect his own skin, or to keep a roof over his head.

Yet the monastic life can never be so "exclusively spiritual" as to preclude all incarnation.

Here, too, would be defection. The monk is bound to remain real, and he cannot be real unless he stays in contact with reality. But reality is, for him, incarnate in God's creation, in the rest of mankind, in its sorrows, it battles, and its perils. Christ, the Word, was made flesh in order to live, suffer, die and rise from death in all men and so deliver them from evil by spiritualizing the material world. The monk remains, then, in a chaotic world of flesh in which he and his Church tirelessly proclaim the primacy of the spirit, but do so by bearing witness to the reality of the Incarnation of the Word. For the monk, and for every Christian, "to live is Christ." The monastic community, as we have said, lives by and for a charity that keeps the *lumen Christi*, the light of Christ, burning in the darkness of an unbelieving world. The monastery is a Tabernacle in which the Most High dwells with men, sanctifying the society of men and uniting them to Himself in His Spirit. The monastic community is dedicated to ceaseless performance of every work of mercy, especially the spiritual works of mercy. The monastery stands, in the sight of the world, as an incomprehensible sacrament of the mercy of God. Incomprehensible, therefore not understood. What is surprising about that? Even the monk himself cannot fully appreciate his own vocation, still less understand it. The mercy of God is in him, nevertheless. Without it, he would be nothing. This is something he cannot help but know, if he is really a monk.

If the monk stands, in some sense, above the divisions of man's society, that does not mean he has no place in the history of nations. He has always been, and always will be, by his vocation, sympathetic to any social and cultural movement that favors the growth of man's spirit. Benedictines have been famous for their humanism and everybody knows that the monks preserved the cultural traditions of antiquity. Wherever a society favors true liberty, monks will be an integral part of that society because the monastery itself is the home of transcendent and spiritual freedom. As such it reproduces on earth the divine charity of which all human freedoms and human communions are but the shadow.

That is why it is important for the monk, above all, to be what he is called, a monk, a solitary, a man made "lonely" by his detachment from all things. But in the loneliness of his detachment he has a far higher vocation to charity than anyone else. For he who has left all things possesses all things, he who has left all men dwells in them all by the charity of Christ, and he who has left even himself for the love of God is capable of working for the salvation of his fellow-man with the irresistible power of God Himself.

INDEX

177